HAI KUAN

THE SEA GATE

海關

by Christopher Briggs MBE

日滋干

AUTHOR'S CHINESE NAME

All foreigners were given a Chinese name on joining the Chinese Maritime Custom. This name was on any document concerning them, such as given in Appendix 4.

Christopher Briggs' Chinese name reads from left to right as PAI LIEH SHIH. The PAI is spoken with a rising tone and the other two are both falling tones.

PAI means White
LIEH means Meritorious or Highly Principled
SHIH means Scholar and also means Gentleman
In South China in Cantonese dialect, the PAI is pronounced as PAK

HAI KUAN
THE SEA GATE
by
Christopher Briggs MBE

Published by Lane Publishers,
61 Charles Street, Stockport, Cheshire SK1 3JR

ISBN 1 897666 36 5

Printed in Great Britain by
Printflow Colour Limited, Bolton BL1 4TH

ACKNOWLEDGMENTS

We acknowledge our thanks to The National Maritime Museum Greenwich for allowing us to print the various photographs, the copyright for which is held by them and may not be copied or reproduced at any time without their prior permission.

This book is dedicated to my late wife Alice (Sis),
who shared with me so many of the years of this story and who,
as a sailor's wife, surmounted very difficult times on her own.

TABLE OF CONTENTS

Glossary 6

Preface 7

Foreword 8

1. On Going To Sea 11

2. Far And Wide 31

3. The Road Home 49

4. New Horizons 59

5. HAI KUAN - The Sea Gate 73

6. New Ships - New places 81

7. The Good Life 87

8. A Year in Shanghai 97

9. North China and Nippon 103

10. A Year at Home 113

11. What Happened to the C.M.C.? 119

Appendix 1   HMS Conway 125

Appendix II.   Flags of China 129

Appendix III.   Customs Ships 130

Appendix IV.   Documents 131

GLOSSARY

Abaft...behind

Aft ....stern end of ship

Backsplice ....end of a rope spliced back into self

Boat falls...ropes for hoisting boats

Bulkhead ....division between compartments

Bunker...fuel storage

C.P.S ....Customs Preventive Ship

Deep Tank ....hold fitted to carry liquids

Forecastle.................................raised portion front of ship

Hove to ....head to wind and sea, speed slow

Serang....................................head of deck\engine. crew

Strake ....row of ship's plating

Watch ....period of duty

Winch ....engine on deck to load cargo

Windlass ....on forecastle for hoisting anchor

PREFACE

My thanks go to those people who helped me in the production of this book. Particularly to my late wife's niece Irene Murray who painstakingly struggled with my writing to put it all on computer and nephew John Murray who has given me such unstinting help with my own computer. To the late Captain W.W.Mortimer for copies of his letters from Captain F.L.Sabel. To Captain T.C.Wan for permission to use his story and to the National Maritime Museum of Britain for their help with documents and photographs. To John Bottomley who has read, edited and advised on the production of this manuscript. I am particularly grateful to Professor Leslie R.Marchant for his excellent Foreword and for the great interest he has taken in my work.

I have called my story HAI KUAN - THE SEA GATE because the most enjoyable years of my life were spent in the service of the Chinese Maritime Customs, whose Chinese characters translated as Sea Gate. Furthermore my training on *HMS CONWAY* was in some way a "sea gate" through which I had to pass before I could reach the sea.

We shall never pass this way again and nothing that I describe in this story will ever be the same - life is different, ships are different - we navigate by pressing a button and our position is shown on a screen. Ships used to be beautiful, now they are often great ugly boxes, sometimes even with square funnels and wharfies drive on and off them with fork lift trucks. I have tried to show what life was like in those days, in some ways harder, in others easier, than life today. The rules were laid down and strictly kept and we never had much money, but we had a lot of fun and there was not much need to worry about the future.

The life of a foreigner in China in the days when Britain was powerful have gone forever - perhaps for the best. China is on its own now and no one knows what its future might be. Her energetic 1.2 billion people are capable of almost anything.

The story of the life and death of *HMS CONWAY*, one time *HMS NILE,* and given in the appendix, is part of the history of the region that is now called Merseyside; of the Menai Strait which divides the mainland on the Cheshire side from the Island of Anglesey, and is crossed by two bridges, one for the railway to Holyhead and the other a road bridge.

More skilled authors than I, such as John Masefield, have had a go at the *Conway* story. I have included the facts of her life and the sad story of the death of this great and beautiful "wooden wall" of old Britain, an early nineteenth century battleship, because it is so very pertinent to my formative years. I have drawn on an article by Leonard G.Fay, MJI, Assoc.INA, for the historical facts of the *Conway* story as given in appendix 1.

I have gone into the history of the Chinese Maritime Customs quite fully. Little appears to have been written about the CMC but I was fortunate to obtain a document entitled "The Chinese Maritime Customs - an International Service" written by B.F.(Dick) Foster-Hall, a one time Commissioner of Customs, from the National Maritime Museum at Greenwich. I have used this extensively in giving an insight into the history of the magnificent Service of which I was so proud to have been a member. I am very grateful to the Museum for their co-operation.

This work is a history of the times and I have used the old and familiar names for places in China.

FOREWORD

The Chinese Maritime Customs was one of the two foreign modelled government departments China was forced to establish after it was opened to foreign trade and intercourse following the so called opium wars. The other office was the Tsung Li Yamen, the bureau of Foreign Affairs, which paved the way for the later Chinese department of Foreign Affairs.

Both developments were deemed essential by Westerners. The Customs service was conceived to provide certainty for foreign merchants who previously faced a confusion of tariff barriers which were difficult to predict, with the added attractive aim of providing the Emperor's government in Peking with a regular income. The Board of Foreign Affairs was designed to better facilitate trade and other treaty negotiations which it handled well, although the foreign powers were never satisfied with it. For after its establishment China lost no territory to the Western powers - only to Japan as a result of its wars. The reversion of Hong Kong to China in 1997 evidences the skills used by officials in the Tsung Li Yamen who worked to preserve the integrity of China while a lot of the rest of continental Asia was being carved up by colonizing powers.

The justification provided for these developments was the thoughts of Adam Smith who envisioned the wealth of nations being multiplied by international trade which would prosper all who engaged in it, and would bring world peace. Hence the treaties made to open China. And hence the coming of the merchants and developers to China who aimed at symbiotic growth with local residents so that Chinese and treaty power merchants could prosper together.

There was, however, a deeper underlying philosophical aim which provided a hidden agenda for China's development. Confucian China, which in the 18th century had been praised and its style emulated in the West where palaces and gardens were adorned with Chinese motifs, in the following century was believed to be disintegrated and weak. It seemed to lack central direction. Provincial officials seemed to hold more sway than those at the capital, Peking. In the view of 19th century Westerners, it needed to be fixed up and given strength and direction. France had manifested the same apparent weakness under the Bourbons. Its 1789 revolutionaries fixed up that. Under the influence of the thoughts of Abbé Sièyes and others, France was created into one nation with one folk with a united economy. The German nation followed suit, organizing itself into a centralized empire under Prussia which built on the base formed by the German Customs Union, *Zollverein*.

It was these models for economic development and modernisation by means of trade, and for centralized national growth which influenced those advising on China's reform, amongst which was what could be called the Cambridge school that included such Chinese reformers as Thomas Wade who played a prominent part in foreign affairs.

The Chinese Maritime Customs was an outstanding model for the movement towards centralization which had not been evident in China since the highly centralized, anti-Confucian Ch'in dynasty which created the Chinese empire out of warring states in the third century BC. The Customs Service's Standards were high. It recruited only the best qualified, and tested these recruits carefully during probationary periods before they were attached to the permanent staff.

When the Service, whose main work was coastal, largely disintegrated as a result of the Japanese invasion of China, and Japan's Pacific war, many of the talented people in the Service together with others such as foreign correspondents and military personnel, shifted to Perth with their families where I found them when I was appointed to teach Chinese studies, University of

Western Australia. There, amongst other purchases, I was fortunate to get from Ireland where the Chinese Customs had personal links in the form of its long time Director Sir Robert Hart, a set of the extensive publications of the Chinese Maritime Customs. These and other original sources provided the means to produce graduates here with first class background knowledge which others who lacked access to such research material could not match. As a bonus, these scholars and I had close at hand with the written sources, a wealth of knowledge and talent in the form of experienced, highly placed officials from the Chinese government service. Captain Christopher Briggs MBE(Mil.), the author of this book about his service in the maritime section of Chinese Maritime Customs, who helped to compile some of the historical sources we acquired, is one of those talented few.

Professor Leslie R.Marchant, Chevalier,
Ordre National du
Mérite; BA(Hons.W.A.) MA(SOAS Lond.) FRGS.

Chapter 1

ON GOING TO SEA

"Good morning Briggs", said the Commissioner of Chinese Maritime Customs, "Welcome to Swatow did you have a good trip?" "Yes, thank you Sir" I replied.

I had joined the *CFS Paktau* in Hong Kong where she had been having her annual refit. She was my first command and I had brought her back to her home base, Swatow. I was very proud of my little ship, even though she was really only a large sea going, steam launch, about 80 feet long.

"Where are you going to live?", asked the Commissioner, one Hughie Hilliard. "On board, I suppose", was my reply. I was not really looking forward to living on board in harbour. Though quite comfortable. I was the only officer. "Would you like to stay with me?. My wife is in England and I have a large house to myself". "Thank you very much, Sir, I would be very grateful" .

I went back to the ship to get my luggage; then our motor boat took me over to the Commissioner's jetty, at the bottom of the garden. The commissioner's lovely house looked out across the river to the town of Swatow.

Swatow was a pretty, sprawling Chinese town, never quiet day or night, about 250 miles North of Hong Kong. Situated a couple of miles up a river, the town and our staff houses were on one side. A fine house for the Commissioner had been built, among other big houses, on the opposite side.

The house was quite delightful. It was really as great honour for me, very junior, to be asked to stay there. I had a big room, one of the servants was detailed to care for me.

My actual boss was the Deputy Commissioner. Anti-smuggling arrangements, there was a lot of smuggling in this district, were part of his duties. English and very friendly, we got on well together.

I had been in Swatow for a couple of weeks. We had made a number of rather unproductive patrols; catching only a small junk with bags of sugar. Our great challenge was to capture a japanese diesel engined fishing boat. We called them 'puff puffs'. They were fitted with a large single cylinder engine and when running, you could hear them miles away, on a still night. They came across from Formosa (now Taiwan) and because they were Japanese we had to be very careful to catch them within the twelve mile limit, or risk an 'incident'.

I was fast asleep when a message came about the expected arrival of a puff puff. No telephone. All messages came by *ting chai*. A boy dressed in white with a red sash and a sailor cap with Chinese Maritime Customs on the band. I signed for the message in the book the boy carried, read it and then sent a message to the ship, to be ready to sail again this evening. I hoped for better luck this time. One of our informers was doing his stuff.

When out of the river we turned right and headed South down the coast towards Hong Kong. When it was quite dark we switched off all our lights and turned North to head for the supposed rendezvous. It was going to be a very dark night, with a calm sea, a slight swell and a light breeze off the land carrying all the scents of China; wood smoke, fragrances, and the smell o f lush vegetation.

Soon we got to where we wanted to be. We settled down to wait with just enough way on to be able to steer. "I think so all right here" said the Coxswain in reply to my query. He knew the area a lot better than I did. The Coxswain was the senior Chinese seaman, a Petty Officer and my second in command. Now the listening started. The crew listened, the engineer came up on deck to listen and I listened all the time and stared through my glasses. About midnight the Coxswain said "I think so puff-puff". I had heard it too. I stopped the engines and tried to decide where the sound was coming from. It seemed to be coming from our starboard quarter so I said "slow ahead hard a-starboard" and we turned slowly towards the sound. We were now heading South and the sound was right ahead. "Half ahead, 20 degrees starboard" and we moved to cut him off. "Full ahead"; a couple of minutes more, "Can see!!" said the coxswain and there was the luminosity of her bow wave and then the boat itself, but heading out to sea. She must have seen us, "damn!!" I said. We raced to cut her off.

We switched on our lights, loaded the 3pdr. gun, opened the shutter of the searchlight and there she was, a fine Formosan (Japanese) fishing trawler, fully loaded and going flat out, but away from us, and the chase began. She was nearly at the twelve mile limit. I ordered "Fire one round ahead". The gunner, a Leading seaman knew just what to do. Aim a little to one side but with enough range to drop the shell ahead of the smugglr. Bang went the 3pdr. but the kept going. I think we are gaining on him. I order one more round from the gun and I pulled on the siren lanyard. The closeness of our shot and the scream of our siren seemed to do the trick, his stern wave died away. "Away motor boat" I ordered. The boat is quickly lowered, as we eased our own speed. Four armed sailors, ready by now with their rifles, jumped down into the boat. Already manned by the boat's coxswain and bowman, they head for our quarry.

I take the ship to within about fifty yards and watch through my glasses. Hard to see what is happening as our boat draws alongside. My sailors start to climb on board, a sudden movement on the deck as one of the crew seemed to move forward holding something above his head, a pistol shot and the man falls. The boat's coxswain, a Leading Seaman, was the only one armed with a pistol, a Webley .45, which he carried tucked into his belt with the lanyard round his neck. The boat returned, leaving four armed sailors as guards on the puff-puff. "Very good full up puff puff" he reported, "Sugar, kerosene, piece goods". These were all highly dutiable. I inquired what had happened. It seemed that as our men moved to board the puff puff, one of her crew rushed forward holding an axe above his head. Without any hesitation the boat's coxswain had shot him. "I think so he kill Tan Ho", our sailor. "Is he dead?" I asked, "I think so", he replied. I commended the seaman for his action which may well have saved one of my sailors from serious injury or death.

I moved the ship closer to the seized vessel, ordered them to head for Swatow and said that we would follow. It was daylight when we entered the river again and an interested group of onlookers turned out to watch. I reported to the Deputy Commissioner. "Well done, Briggs, I am glad you got a big one at last", he said. "I am afraid that the boat's crew had to shoot one of the puff puff men" I reported. "One of the crew rushed forward with an axe to attack the boarding party". "Don't worry about it", he said. "Leave it to me and the Chinese police". I never heard any more about it. " A couple of days off would do us a lot of good", I thought. That was the second one we had caught. The first had been much easier.

All that was well into my journey through life. This was how it all began .

A 14 year old sat in a third class carriage on a train from London to Liverpool. It was September 1921 and he was on his way to the Mercantile Marine training ship *HMS CONWAY* anchored off Rock Ferry, on the Birkenhead side of the river Mersey. He was dressed in a naval cadet uniform of blue reefer jacket, with 8 brass buttons and one small button on each lapel with the blue cord of a Royal Naval Reserve Cadet. Blue trousers, black shoes and peaked cap with the Royal Naval badge, a blue shirt, white stiff collar and black tie completed the outfit. The uniform had a certain newness about it denoting a first-termer or new boy. The boy was me.

I had wanted to join the Royal Navy but the year 1920 when I was 13 1/2 was one of the worst years for the Navy, ever. Cadet training at Osborne, Isle of Wight, had been closed down, Officers were being retired in hundreds, as the "War to End All Wars" had finished two years before. Armies and navies were not going to be needed any more. My desire was still to go to sea, so after another year at school it was decided that I should join the Mercantile Marine or Merchant Navy as it is usually referred to nowadays.

I was not brought up in luxury but certainly in comfort and all his life my father, Philip Lemuel Briggs, had enough private income to live on without having to work. Looking back I would say that this robbed the country of the services of an intelligent and thinking man, well educated and well read. It was the custom of his time and his class not to work if the income was not needed. Certainly not in commerce, though a profession was an exception, as were the armed Services.

My great grandfather, Christopher Briggs, was a lawyer in Bolton, Lancashire and at one time the law firm in Wood Street was called Briggs and Bailey. Later it became Fullagar, Hulton and Bailey and then Hulton and Bailey. My grandfather Arthur Lemuel Briggs did not take up law but went into the cotton business. He married an Ormrod, which may have brought him money and together with others he founded the company called Fine Cotton Spinners, which I believe is alive today. The firm was designed to cash in on the demand for special cotton needed for the machine made lace on the continent of Europe. My grandfather was interested in politics and for some time was the chairman of the Bolton Conservative Council.

Arthur Lemuel Briggs died in one of the early influenza epidemics at the age of 47 and though his Will gave the disposition of a very large capital, his fortunes at the time of his death were at a low ebb and instead of riches the family were left just well off.

My grandmother left Bolton and retired to Hereford with her two younger children Godfrey and Cordelia. My father was a cadet at Sandhurst. I always understood that he had joined the Army against his will and had wanted to join the Navy. However on the death of his father he left the Army and got enough money from his mother to go to Canada where he bought or rented a place on the Bow River outside Calgary.

He was a fine horseman and settled down to breed racehorses and be his own trainer and jockey. I still have his green and white racing colours. He was a smallish, lightly built man and used to ride 7 stone 7 lbs (44 kilograms).

Philip Briggs' life in Canada was that of an Englishman who had to have everything as it would have been at home. He imported the first pack of English fox hounds to Western Canada, though there were no foxes to hunt. The coyote was an adequate substitute. The mounted head of one of these wolf-like animals remained with him until we cleared his home after his death in 1947.

The other importation was polo. I doubt that there was much played at that time. Before me is a plated tankard with a glass bottom. 1893 Regina Polo Cup. P.L. Briggs - T. O. Critchley - O. A. Critchley - C. G. Ross, and underneath the names the initials PLB are monogrammed. In later years the Critchleys were to become well known in England, especially for their participation in greyhound racing. George Ross became the manager of a ranch, owned by the Prince of Wales, later King Edward VIII, outside Calgary. Another of my father's friends was a Bob Milvain. He was one of my godfathers and had been on the gold rush to the Klondyke, with some success.

In 1898 my father married Beatrice Amy Vaughan of Millom, Cumberland. I do not know the circumstances of their meeting but I always understood that it was through my father's brother Godfrey. He had met my mother on a liner voyage to South Africa. Father made periodical trips from Canada to England with racehorses and the meeting must have taken place during one of those trips.

My mother was a good horsewoman too. She smoked cigarettes when this was by no means the general rule and she knew how to manage a large household. The details of cooking had not been necessary knowledge and her early days in Canada were difficult to say the least. After the wedding my father and mother returned to Canada and the ranch on the Bow River at Calgary. The conditions, I would think, were quite beyond her imagination. She left a large two storey house in Millom with coachhouses, coachman, grooms, gardeners, servants and all the trappings of the Victorian well to do.

The house on the Bow River was a single storey weatherboard house, on the prairie and some distance from Calgary. She had a Chinese cook and my father had at least one man to help him with the horses. Everyone had to be fed by my mother and the cook. She learned quickly and in the years to come was a very good natural cook. I remember watching her in later years making a cake from memory with a cigarette in her mouth and the ash getting longer and longer. Just as the ash was about to fall into the mix she would flick it to some more suitable spot.

The summers were hot and refrigeration was unheard of and the winters were cold, very cold. The temperature would go down at times to 40F below zero. The men used to wear felt lined boots when cleaning out the stables and would then put the damp boots to dry on the back of my mothers stove, thereby adding the smell of horse manure to the kitchen smells. I don't think she was ever happy there and it was a period of her life she never talked about very much.

My mother was unfortunate with her pregnancies and lost two babies in the hospital at Winnipeg. This must have been a great disappointment to her and I think must have turned her away from Canada altogether, because my father left the ranch and returned to England with the idea of going into the racehorse business. This never materialised. My father wanted to start at the bottom and learn the racehorse game but his friends wanted him at the top; a gentleman could not actually work. He gave up easily and they went to live in the West of Ireland. To add to my mother's disappointment, twins(a boy and girl), died when about six weeks old. They had been born at Millom and are buried in the churchyard there.

I was born some years later. A brother-in-law of my mother's was a doctor and lived in Cowes, Isle of Wight. My Aunt and Uncle insisted that my mother went to stay with them before her time. This seemed to have been a success and I was a large healthy baby and there were no problems.

One of the more interesting features of NW England was the Hodbarrow Iron Mine at Millom of which my maternal grandfather, Cedric Vaughan, was the managing director. At his death my uncle George Vaughan became the MD until the mine was finally closed. The full story of the Hodbarrow mine is given in the book Cumberland Iron by A. Harris published by D. Bradford Barton Ltd, Truro. During the lifetime of the mine, over a century from 1855 to 1968, the mine produced 20 million tons of high grade haematite ore. Situated on the North side of the Duddon estuary and close to Millom the proximity to the sea enabled the ore to be shipped out in small coastal sailing vessels with names such as Donald and Doris, Happy Harry, which

Calgary. The house and stables.

Calgary. P. L. Briggs, standing. Mr. & Mrs. Critchley.

were eventually sold. However some customers in Scotland continued to obtain their supplies of ore by sea until 1940

The iron ore deposit was found to run out under the sea and over the years barriers, or sea walls had been built to keep the sea away from the area over that being mined. During the building of the second of these sea walls one of the young engineers became engaged to one of my mother's sisters. Later he moved to building wharves in Hong Kong and Shanghai where they lived for some years.

The latter years of the mine were ones of great struggle and adversity. Rising costs, the constant battle against the sea and the failure to find new payable ore bodies put an end in 1968 to one of the more colourful sagas of iron mining in Britain.

20 million tons of high grade iron ore was quite a large tonnage for an underground mine worked by hand. My Uncle George Vaughan did introduce small diesel locos for work underground hauling skips of ore. One of the large iron-ore mines in Western Australia ship out as much ore as this total in a couple of years.

My mother was one of a family of nine - 5 girls, 4 boys. One of the girls and two of the brothers married doctors. The most distinguished of the family was the brother Louis. He became Major-General Sir Louis Vaughan, and made his name during the 1914-18 war. After the war he served in India for some years before retiring and joining Sir Alfred Mond later Lord Melchett in business. The unusual number of doctors who married into the family is due to the eldest sister Ethel. She was one of the pioneers of women in medicine and finally became Dr.Ethel Vaughan-Sawyer, a specialist gynaecologist who lived all her working life at 131 Harley Street. She had married Major Harry Sawyer who was killed in France in 1914. During her student years she must have introduced her brothers and sisters to her fellow students, resulting in the various marriages. Ethel was very fond of my mother and we always stayed with her in Harley Street whenever we were in London.

My parents were well educated - for their day - and very well read. Possibly having enough money to live on was my father's greatest handicap. In later years his income had shrunk so much that living was difficult for them in their old age.

At the time I was born my parents were moving to a house called Liskilleen at Balinrobe in the West of Ireland, very close to two lovely lakes, Lough Corrib and Lough Mask. My father loved fishing and this was the reason they took this house on what I think must have been a five or six year lease.

After my birth in Cowes, mother took me to her parents home at Millom. It seems that after some time there mother went to Ireland leaving me with my nanny. Once my parents had settled into the new house I was sent for and my nanny took me by ship from Heysham in Lancashire to Dublin and on to Ballinrobe. We settled in and it was at Liskilleen that my early years, with the beginnings of memory were spent.

We had not been there very long when mother had an afternoon tea party and one of the ladies said "Oh Mrs Briggs, I'm sure we saw your pram and your baby outside the pub in the village when we came past". My pram would have been very noticeable. That was the end of that nanny, the one that had brought me over from England.

When I was about 10 or 12 years old I told my mother of a memory that I had and often wondered about. I remembered quite vividly being carried along a covered area near the sea and down some steps into water. Then being pulled out, taken on board a ship and wrapped in a blanket, there were people all round. That was the memory, and I was a baby in arms.

Author with mother and nanny.

At Liskilleen. Author with parents and 'Duchess'.

Mother was pretty puzzled about this and had no answer except that it was something that had happened when I was with my nanny on the journey from Millom to Ireland. She told me that the next time she had been to Millom the servants said "We're glad Master Christopher got to Ireland safely because his nanny was so drunk when she left here that she could hardly stand". No one thought of telling my grandmother but I suppose there is a loyalty among servants.

Some years later when I had been staying with father's family in Lancashire, I went back to Ireland via Heysham, which was nearer than Liverpool, and a ship went daily to Dublin. There was the covered concrete decked pier, just as I remembered. Owing to a large rise and fall of the tide, the pier had two decks and, 'lo and behold', there were the steps leading down into the water as the tide was up and the ship was alongside at the top level, just as I remembered. It is amazing that the incident should have sunk into the brain of a child only months old. I do not know exactly how old I was. Other memories do not begin until I was four or five years old.

Liskilleen was haunted, quite haunted. It was a beautiful ivy covered house with a long tree lined drive in from the road, and a large gravel area by the front door, large enough to turn round a horse and carriage. To the left of the house was the drawing room with the large hall and staircase in the centre, and the dining room on the right. My father had a room on the left, and above th is was my parents bedroom and a guest room. The drawing room had two big windows with double sashes on counterweights looking out to the garden. The windows were large and low and if you raised the bottom sash you could step out into the garden. Over the dining room was my day nursery and I suppose a bedroom for me and my nanny at the back. The kitchen was downstairs and the servants rooms upstairs. We usually kept a nanny or governess for me, a cook, a house parlourmaid, and a gardener. (A house parlourmaid is a parlourmaid who does housework in addition to waiting at table and so on).

There was no doubt about the haunting. A young woman in white was often seen in the drive. My father used to hear someone running on the landing at the top of the stairs, and then a scream and a thud. Legend had it that a woman had jumped from the landing down into the hall, some 12 feet or so, and was killed. Sometimes my father would hear one of the big windows in the drawing room being flung open. On going down he would find one of his carefully locked windows open and the curtains blowing in the night breeze. He would shut the window and go back to bed. This never worried my mother or my father but it was a different "kettle of fish" for my Aunt Corrie, my fathers sister. She used to come from England to stay. She was a bit "fey" and one of the people for whom spirits will materialise. My Aunt always brought her fox terrier with her and she would put an open bible on her bed when she went down to dinner and it was always closed when she came back to her bedroom. The terrier could sense something too and would watch things in the room and growl. My poor Aunt never stayed long and years after said to me "I don't know how your father could stand that awful house".

We had a beautiful black labrador called Duchess. She was the same age as me and lived until I went to school, when she had to be put down. I must have been about three, when Duchess had a litter of puppies. She had a nest in one of the loose boxes in the stable. One day one of the maids went to my mother and said "Master Christopher is in the stable with the bitch and her puppies and she won't let us go near her to get him to come in for his tea". I suppose when my mother called me I just went to her and anyway Duchess would not mind her near the puppies.

During our last year at Liskilleen I remember one afternoon I was in my nursery and they explained to me that a large liner had hit an iceberg and sunk and that many people were drowned. I remember it quite clearly and of course it would have been the Titanic and I was five

Tully Lodge.

'Puggy,' the 1912 Peugeot.

in 1912. My next memory of that time was a furniture van loading outside the front of the house. I remember taking a model crane I had made out of Meccano out to the men and asking them to put it in the van. Soon we were off to our next house in Ireland, Tully Lodge in the village of Kilmore near Drumsna in County Roscommon. A lovely house I was to remember well and we were there for seven years to 1919.

Tully was a well built, warm, dry and convenient house- except there was a long walk from the kitchen at the back to the dining room at the front and it was not haunted. My bedroom, after I started school, was the room with the three windows over the entrance hall (see photograph). It had a lovely view over open country studded with trees and green, the lovely deep green of Ireland, no wonder green is the National colour. Mother's bedroom upstairs on the left and father's on the right. Both these rooms had large dressing rooms attached. Downstairs on the left was the drawing room and on the right the dining room off a large tiled central hall with the staircase leading up. A long passage led from the hall to the kitchen. I was able to ride my pedal vehicle down the passage, round the kitchen table and back up the passage. Off this passage my father had two rooms one as a study and the other was his gunroom. Then a large kitchen with pantry, scullery and more store cupboards and last but certainly not least was a huge black coal fired range with a hot water boiler behind the fire. Upstairs on the left a spare room used for linen, sewing, ironing etc. and opposite a large bathroom and lavatory. On down the passage and on the left was a large room which had been my night nursery when I was small and also for my governess. Across the back of the house was a fine warm room over the kitchen which was my day nursery and became my playroom after I went to school. The house was narrower at the back and my playroom had two windows, one looked out over the garden, and the other looked out over the courtyard at the back of the house. This courtyard was a stable yard with buildings on three sides and contained a dairy, harness, room cart shed, coal store etc. The house was modern for the period with running hot and cold water and an inside toilet upstairs and another downstairs for the servants . The water supply was good and came from a spring fed reservoir on top of the hill behind the house . It is said that it is only in Ireland that you would find a spring on top of a hill!!. The dairy was a cool place, with a red tiled floor. A line of stone shelves ran round the walls, upon which stood large low enamel pans in which the milk was allowed to stand. The cream was skimmed off at night or next morning. Cream separators were not common then. The property consisted of about twenty acres with large formal and vegetable gardens to the left of the house. Away from the house was a large farmyard with cowsheds, piggery, stables, hay shed and so on. This we let to a local farmer as we were not in the business of farming, except that we had a couple of cows and my donkey which we kept there. There was also a beautiful one acre walled paddock, very sheltered, and some years we put in potatoes there.

I suppose when you are brought up in these conditions it is easy to acquire a love of the country. There is so much for a kid to do and it is all free. When I was nine my father gave me a .22 rifle and taught me to use it, clean it, protect it and all the safety rules. When I came home after rabbiting, usually with four or five dead rabbits, I had to clean my rifle to his satisfaction and then it was locked away in the gun case. I had to ask for it the next time I wanted to take it out. A never to be forgotten training and I have always been very careful of weapons all my life.

Even though I was an only child I never remember being bored or lonely. Before I went to school I always had a governess. Then I tried bringing a boy home from school for the holidays but this was not a great success. I suppose I wasn't used to sharing my things with anyone.

It could have been from this time that my interest in cooking began. Servants came and servants went. Occasionally we had none because replacements had to be engaged from Dublin and that always took a little time. Local help, untrained, was available daily if required and we usually had someone in for the rough cleaning anyway. When servantless, mother and I would get up, about six, and the first thing we did was light the big black range and get a roaring fire going so there was hot water for father's bath when he got up.

Servants are of course a mixed blessing. One day my mother asked what had happened to the roast beef that was left over from Sunday. The cook replied "I'm sorry mam, the bitch got it off the kitchen table and when I saw her she had it 'that dragged' it was only fit for the master's sandwiches" (the bitch was a big golden Labrador we had then)

At Tully we were away from the lakes and close to the River Shannon. The fishing was not good, trout fishing that is, there were too many coarse fish, pike and perch. My father now invested in a car. He bought a 1912 Peugeot two seater, we called it 'Puggy', it was his pride and joy. Shining brass radiator, one huge brass headlight with a carbide gas burner and two oil side lamps, brass horn, wooden spoked wheels, comfortable leather seats. No electrics of course and a magneto for the spark plugs. He went by train to Dublin to get it and then drove home, quite a long way. I know it took four hours in the train as I always came home that way and father would meet me at Drumsna station.

In those days the village shops were just that - village shops - so nearly everything had to come from Dublin. The weekly laundry went to Dublin in a large basket and was picked up from the station a week later and another despatched. All our household stores came from Dublin every month. My father used to get beer in a small 4 1/2 gallon barrel called a "pin" and occasionally oysters arrived in a small wooden tub with the oysters packed in seaweed.

One morning at breakfast my father appeared with a face that looked rather sore and he had no eyebrows. My inquiry as to his welfare brought no response except "Shut up". Later Mother explained that my father had been out at night in the car and when he left to go home he turned on the water drip in the big brass headlight to activate the carbide. I suppose people were talking so he forgot about it for a while then struck a match to light the lamp and "whoosh", a sheet of flame and no eyebrows on papa. He was lucky he hadn't damaged his eyes.

My father had a plan for me. He was very pro-Roman Catholic and wanted me to go to a Convent primary school and then to Clongoes, the famous Catholic school that has turned out so many Irish priests. Mother put her foot down and won the day. I went to one of a number of English run preparatory schools in the Dublin area; Monkstown Park School at Monkstown just South of Dublin and about 30 minutes in a tram from central Dublin. It was a small school of about sixty boys, run by Mr Bentley and his sister with two permanent masters and various visiting teachers for music and so on. I got on very well there and stayed there for five years including the war years, 1914-18.

The large grey school house stood on a low hill overlooking extensive grounds. On the valley floor below were our playing fields and a cottage in which the two masters lived. On the other side of the valley and up a slight rise was a house for boarders.. The school classrooms all being in the big house. There were a number of similar schools in the area, so it was possible to arrange a program of sports fixtures with them for cricket, hockey, and football. We could swim in the sea in summer and there was a good swimming spot within walking distance.

Every Sunday we walked in a 'crocodile' to Monkstown Church. A very fine large Anglican Church or Church of Ireland as it was then called. It stands today, just off the main road from Dublin to Dunlaoghaire, which in my day was called Kingstown. We would all be given a penny to put in the collection and the thing to do was to try and change this for two halfpennies. One halfpenny went in the collection, and on the way back to school you could nip into a little shop and spend the other halfpenny, on sweets. You could actually buy something for a halfpenny in those days.

In the grounds of the school near the house was a tower built of stone, in a triangular form. Quite tall with stone steps inside, from the top there was a good view of Dublin, Dublin Bay and Howth Head.

Even though many of the boys were either English or of English descent we were all fiercely pro-Irish, whenever there was some incident which resulted in a battle between police and Sein Fein we would shout "Up the Rebels". Occasionally my father and mother came to Dublin and always took rooms in the same house in Merrion Square. When they stayed over a weekend I was allowed out from school to stay with them. One night there was a well known incident in which the rebels raided houses where they knew British Army Officers were staying and a number of Officers and their wives were murdered. The house next door but one was raided. There must have been a gun battle because next morning I was thrilled to find empty cartridge cases on the pavement and in the gutter. Relics I gleefully took back to school on Sunday night.

There is an Irish song beginning "Who fears to speak of Easter Week". This refers to the Irish rebellion of Easter 1916 when much of central Dublin was destroyed and Nelson's Column in O'Connell Street got badly scarred. The main battle took place in and around the G.P.O. which was shelled from the sea by British warships. Easter used to come during the school holidays but this year the fighting was on in Dublin and only those of us who lived South of Dublin could go home. I had to cross Dublin to get to Amiens Street station to catch the train to the West. Though most of the school were able to go home, about a dozen or so of us were stuck at school over Easter. Our main occupation was standing up in the tower watching the battle. At night it was quite spectacular, especially when the occasional shell was lobbed towards the G.P.O. from the sea. Eventually the rebellion collapsed and we were all allowed to go home. When I passed the smoking ruins of the G.P.O. and O'Connell Street, I got my first sight of what the aftermath of war can look like.

This was the beginning of a very sad time in Ireland which barely ended with the granting of Home Rule in 1927. When the war ended in 1918 the British Government recruited special police for Ireland. They wore a khaki uniform with a black police cap. They were called the "black and tans" and were well and truly hated by the people. Groups of these ex-soldiers used to ride round the countryside in trucks, all armed, interrogating and arresting people Quite a number of people were murdered, "for resisting arrest". Houses were burnt and cattle shot in an effort to keep the people thoroughly cowed. Of course it did not work and the people were only more determined to get their freedom from the hated British. .

All this did not effect us very much at Tully Lodge. I was going to school and the holidays were spent boating with my father, shooting rabbits with my .22. It was fairly lonely because there was only one family with children of my age in the neighbourhood. The boating on Lough Boderg was what I enjoyed most. We had a boatshed on the lake shore and two boats. The sailing boat was about 20 feet, with a drop keel and half decked, and was moored just off our boatshed. The other was a rowing boat with an Evinrude outboard motor. Very primitive single cylinder, a magneto under the flywheel which was on top with a handle to spin the fly wheel to start. Sometimes it did and sometimes, exasperatingly, it didn't. My father had strengthened the boat's transom to take the motor and all went well. The snag, however, was that the rowing boat of those days had a big 'rise of floor' at the after end, so when under way with the engine going and my father sitting beside it steering the bow stuck up in the air and I had to sit in the bow to try to keep it down a bit. He realized he should have a boat specially built for an outboard engine. There should be no 'rise of floor' or narrowing to the stern with the large transom going down to the level of the keel. Quite a new design for those days. Father got a boat builder at Mullingar to build exactly to our design. The boat duly arrived, towed by a motor barge all the way from Mullingar on Ireland's magnificent inland waterways. The new boat was a great success. We won a number or races on L. Boderg, held by the North Shannon Yacht Club once a year!

Adjoining L. Boderg to the East was L. Bofin. In the other direction was the town of Carrick on Shannon. There was a lock and a weir between us and Carrick to adjust the river level to keep it navigable. We used to go shopping in Carrick by boat and visiting friends who lived in the few big houses on the shores of the two lakes. Ireland is the land of lakes and quite close to our house there was a small lake by which we used to picnic in summer and in which I taught myself to swim and to fish for perch. Others used to swim in the lake too. One day our old gardener, Masterson, said to my mother that he had been down to the lake that morning and seen the parson swimming, adding "Saving your honour's presence, he was as naked as the day he was born".

One cold night in winter and pouring rain there was a knock on the front door. My mother went to answer it and I followed. A middle aged woman wrapped up in a black shawl stood there with a tiny goat in her arms. "Would your honour buy the wee kid, we have no money in the house?" Pushed by me, my mother said yes. I don't know how much she paid, not more than two shillings, I expect. The goat, a nanny, became my pet and when she grew bigger I made a cart for her. She came for walks, came mushrooming; she liked mushrooms and it was a race to get one before the goat. We used to sit in front of the house in deck chairs in the sun, the goat beside us quietly chewing her cud. After a while she would sometimes have a small pile of plum stones. We knew she had been in the orchard standing up on her hind legs to eat green plums.

We were English people and we lived in a large house. We had sporting arms and ammunition two 12 bore shotguns and two .22 rifles - one was mine. One had the feeling that things were getting tense as the push for home rule became more strident. One night father went to answer the front door and wrapped in one of the ubiquitous black shawls was the wife of the licensee of one of the two pubs in the village. She said she had come "To tell your honour that there are some of the boys down from Dublin and they are talking about raiding Mr Briggs for arms". The lady was suitably thanked as what she had done was not without a great element of risk. We were not raided after all and very soon the lease of Tully expired and we left Ireland forever. We went to Jersey of all places. I had come to love Ireland and its people. For their sufferings under the years of British rule they have my sympathy.

To become an officer in the British Mercantile Marine, now referred to as the Merchant Navy, and sadly reduced to a shadow of its former self, it was necessary to serve a 4 year apprenticeship in sea going ships. However, if a boy did 2 years on one of the training ships *HMS Conway* in the Mersey at Liverpool, *HMS Worcester* in the Thames at London, or Pangbourne Nautical College, the apprenticeship was reduced to three years. These training establishments were quite expensive with the added cost of uniforms but the great advantage was that the boy could start at 14, go to sea at 16 and have his Second Mates Certificate before he was 20.

The *Conway* was chosen for me on the advice of my Uncle Frank, the RN Commander, and I now embarked on one of the less enjoyable periods of my life. Subject to colds and tonsil

H.M.S. Conway in the Mersey on the Rock Ferry.

On the rocks in the Menai Strait.

trouble, a bit chesty, I spent the next two years on a ship anchored on the muddy waters of the Mersey under the almost eternally grey skies of what is now called Merseyside. The ship was anchored to two anchors on the river bed. One upstream and one downstream. Two chain cables led up to a swivel and then one cable from each bow of the ship led down to the swivel. The ship could therefore swing freely to the tide. She even used to roll a little at the change of the tide if she was heading across the river and there was a real winter Westerly gale blowing at the time. We had plenty of these. Memories of my arrival on board are hazy. The trip from the Liverpool landing stage, on the ferry to Rock Ferry pier, took 30 minutes. There we would have been met by the *Conway's* big motor boat manned by two disdainful cadets and the ship's engineer we called "Fat Jack". We never knew his proper name. New chums were regarded as the lowest of the low.

Within certain limits a term of new entrants worked and stayed together for the two years. We became 1st termers, 2nd termers and so on up to 6th - the last term. Privileges began as 3rd termers but more of that later.

My term were all placed in a division called Starboard Fore. There were six divisions or "tops" as they were called. Port and Starboard Fore, Port and Starboard Main and Port and Starboard Mizzen. When I arrived at the part of the ship that was allocated to Starboard Fore, there was my large black sea chest, with my name painted in white standing against the ships side. There was much to learn that first day and the first was how to sling a hammock. There was a hook on a beam at the ships, side about four feet from the deck, and a metal strut which was hooked up to the deckhead when not in use some ten feet inboard from the hook. The hammock was a simple canvas rectangle with sewn eyelets each end. Cords called "nettles" went from each eyelet to a ring, and a length of rope was spliced into the ring so that the hammock could be slung 'feet' towards the ship's side and 'head' inboard. A small mattress went with the hammock together with a pillow, sheets and blankets. My first night in a hammock was strange but one soon got used to them and my memory goes back to many warm and cosy nights wrapped up tightly; the sides of the hammock protecting the sleeper from any draft. At first we were not allowed to have stretchers to keep the sides of the hammock apart. This was allowed to third termers and above. Two short lengths of batten, with grooved ends fitted neatly at head and foot kept the hammock open.

At some unearthly hour of the morning when one was dead to the world came 'reveille' on the bugle followed by shouts of the duty Petty Officer "Wakey - Wakey, Rise and Shine", and out you had to get, sometimes in the miserable cold of a Liverpool winter's morning.

The Conway was the old wooden four deck battleship *HMS Nile*. She must have been a rare sight in her day - under full sail. She was painted black with the strake★ of ports at the main deck painted white.

The Upper Deck was the top open deck with the high poop aft covering the Captain's quarters and from which the ship would have been navigated. There was beautiful carved woodwork and teak rails on the poop, a large brass compass binnacle and huge wooden steering wheel. Plenty of brass to polish. Brass odds and ends seemed to be everywhere. Forward was the raised forecastle with two huge spare anchors with wooden stocks. The forecastle contained the lavatories and there was a single boiler in a boiler house just abaft the forecastle. This small marine type boiler supplied power for the electric generators, galleys and the coaling winch. The lavatories were always referred to as the "heads", and are still the "heads" today in H.M. Ships wherever they are situated. The reason being that they were under the forecastle head. Senior boys used them for a quick smoke!!. The main deck was the next one down, beautifully scrubbed

---

★ Falls: ropes to hoist and lower boats

to the whitest. The woodwork was painted white. The large brass bell was always well polished. The gratings over the hatchways were well scrubbed. On each side were large square ports. It was our parade deck where we mustered for divisions, prayers, church, meals, school, dancing or any occasion when we all needed to be on deck together. It always seemed so bright and clean and sometimes the river and the land, only a few houses then, could look lovely in the sunshine. Mess tables with folding legs were secured to the deck head and were lowered and set up for meals and school. The galley was forward and was of good size to cater for some 190 boys for three meals a day.

The lower deckwas very much a working deck. Right forward were rows of washbasins, bathrooms and some lavatories which were for use at night. Aft were the Officers' and Padre's cabins and the canteen. Amidships was the permanent gangway. All the boats falls★ were led into the lower deck, and it was from there that the boats were hoisted and lowered. The "still" would be sounded and "hands to hoist motorboat", or whichever, would be piped. Then there would be a rush to man the falls laid out along the deck. Then the orders "take the weight, hoist away" and up the boat would come at the double. Any pipe such as for hoisting boats or clearing lower decks meant a rush for the hatchway ladders. The presence of a Petty Officer at the bottom of the ladder armed with a long cane, which they used indiscriminately on anyone slow to move, was an incentive to keep at the double.

The next deck down was the Orlop deck. This deck was used for sleeping. Rows of sea chests stood along the ships side and the hammocks were stowed in racks. There was a large heating furnace about midships on this deck. In winter it did give some heat, but my memories of two winters is mostly of being cold.

Under the Orlop deck was the hold. There was a flat used by the Cadet Captains in the hold. We had access to the lower hold and we used it as a place of quiet.I have recollections of repairing to the hold with a tin of pineapple or a tin of baked beans. Some idea of the massive timbers used in the framework of the ship, and the size of the keelson could be gained in the hold.

Ashore, not far from Rock Ferry pier, was Conway House and our playing fields. The house was used as a hospital for anyone too ill for the sick bay on board and for convalescents. The playing fields were used frequently. Rugby football in winter, cricket and tennis in summer. We may have played hockey.

We were well off for boats. Our complement consisted of one large motor boat - the steam pinnace had gone by 1921 - two twelve oared cutters, a four oared Captain's gig, and two sailing dinghies. The latter were exactly the same and were named "Taw" and "Torridge", after two west country rivers. This enabled us to sail these two boats in competition. Boat sailing in the Mersey was not all that simple. The tide at times runs at some knots and squalls come suddenly. It was important to keep upstream of the ship so that it was possible to get back to the ship on the tide. I once upset my dinghy in a squall and the three of us had a wet and chilly time in the river until the motor boat came to pick us up and tow the dinghy back. No one was very pleased.

Rowing in a twelve oared cutters crew was something that needed practice. The boats were heavy. So were the oars. I used to enjoy it, though I was rather a weedy lad and never heavy enough to be chosen for a racing cutters crew. A cutter was often used in bad weather, with a special crew. It was presumed to be more reliable than the motor boat. On the flood tide it was downhill all the way from the ferry pontoon to the ship which was moored upstream. With a strong ebb tide - and they were strong - the cutter would work upstream close to the shore and out of the tide until well upstream of the ship and then work across the tide without losing too much ground to reach the gangway.

Boatwork was one of the invaluable aspects of training in this type of schoolship. The apprentice who goes straight to sea in an ocean going ship never gets, in his whole training, the almost daily use of boats. He may get the occasional use of a lifeboat on an exercise in harbour - if there is time - but never the constant use of boats for everything. Quite recently I saw in a magazine an article on sea training which said "Lack of practical boatwork experience is something of which we are very well aware at sea and we do use what opportunities we have, but have to remember that if a lifeboat is damaged it is a big expense and a big problem". Training in small boats taught us to be careful and to remember that the sea is a dangerous and very unforgiving element.

One was well aware of the danger when watching a strong ebb tide rushing past the old *Conway,* especially when there was a Westerly Gale against it to kick up quite a sea.

The stewards and cooks ran various rackets, which meant a little extra cash for them and a little extra food for us. Normally, at mid morning break we mustered for a mug of cocoa and a hardtack biscuit. If, however, you had paid the steward 2s/6d at the beginning of the term one got a sandwich instead of hardtack. The cooks had their chance by offering a Sunday night supper which cost 5s/- a term. It was a good hot supper and worth the money. Money was tight as far as I was concerned, so I never felt able to subscribe to these extras. The *Conway* fee was just over £46 per term plus the cost of clothes and pocket money. It was quite a tidy annual sum for those days. My father, who lived on a fixed and diminishing income, grumbled continuously. So in later life, when I wanted to leave the sea, his resistance can perhaps be understood.

One night after I had been in the ship about a year - I remember it was summer; three of us decided to raid the pantry. We spent some time puzzling out how this could be done. The pantry was on the main deck some 40-50 feet or more forward of the starboard gangway. The main deck ports were large and square and quite big enough to climb in and out of. The ports were covered by a pair of casement windows opening out and two long metal hooks were fitted to rings so that the ports could be secured open or V-ed so that they were partially open for ventilation. If the two sides were closed together they met and formed a V; to close the port the two sides had to be shut one at a time. The lower deck was used at night because of the night use lavatories in the forward part. No notice would be taken of a boy on the lower deck at night. Our observations showed that, if the weather was fine, the stewards always V-ed the two pantry ports when they finished at night. Inspection also showed that due to the tumble-home (the ship was wider at the water line than at the upper deck giving a pot bellied effect) of the ships side, and a narrow ledge running along just below the ports, it was possible to get out of the port nearest the pantry, move along and then unhook the pantry port and get inside. The right night arrived, fine and a little wind. I do not know what time it was, but the ship had settled down for the night when two of us made our raid on the pantry. We filled a pillow case with bread, butter, and sugar which we stowed in our sea chests and ate at leisure for some days after. When I think of it now and look back at the rushing Mersey tide, I think with horror what would have happened if one of us had slipped on our journey outside the ships side. There were no complaints from the stewards but we noticed that the pantry ports were closed at night from then on.

There was a certain amount of bullying but it was mild, not excessive, and quickly dealt with by the Cadet Captains when noticed. New chums came off worst as could be expected. Running silly errands was commonplace at first. Some senior hand would send a new chum to the store for some "Duresco" for the Last Post. "Duresco" was a kind of whitewash which was much used on the ships interior of hold and orlop decks. Of course there was also the old gag of the green oil for the starboard light.

Cadet Captains were allowed to carry a "teaser". This consisted of a short length of cord with a backplice on one end about three inches to give it weight and a loop for the wrist at the other. Should a Cadet Captain sight some minor misdemeanour, the culprit would be ordered to bend over and summary justice would be done to the extent of a few cuts with the teaser, say one to three. Gross misconduct meant a visit to the Cadet Captains quarters where a trial was held and more severe punishment was decided upon. It all worked very well, and I don't remember any cases of injustice or of major offences which had to go to the Commander. I think we were very well behaved. We learned to obey orders at once. Jump to it and do things at the double. There was no argument - an order was given and you did it at once. It was good discipline and I have never ever had difficulty taking orders from seniors or of giving them; as one learned this too.

My mother suggested that I should learn to dance. It was an extra, but in my last year I joined the class which was held once a week. The main deck was rigged for dancing with a screen across just forward of the mainmast to make it a bit private. The dancing instructress arrived with a couple or so of young women to help. We were dressed in our best. The piano was rolled out and off we went. I enjoyed it and learned the basics of rhythm and some simple steps. This stood me in good stead later on and I loved dancing ever after. Many years later I met a lady in Perth, Western Australia, who was interested in and knew a lot about the *Conway*. When asked why this was, she told me she knew the dancing instructress, and used to go off to the ship as one of the dancing partners when the ship was in the Menai Strait. No wonder she knew so many 'Old Conways'.

It was unfortunate that I had to miss a term because of illness. We lived in a little village on the Welsh coast called Aberayron, fifteen miles South of Aberystwyth. The train journey from Liverpool was a slow and complicated one. Though Aberayron was on the railway, this came from the South whereas, the train from Liverpool came to an end at Aberystwyth. The day journey got me into Aberystwyth too late to continue, so I was allowed to catch a night train from Liverpool, as were others with long or difficult journeys. Returning home for Christmas, at the end of my 4th term I had a cold journey in a barely heated 3rd class carriage. I arrived at Aberystwyth about 6.30 am or so and as usual got a lift with the little green van which picked up the morning newspapers for delivery on the road to Aberayron The van was colder still, and shortly after I got home I became very ill. My knees swelled up and the doctor said I had an acute rheumatic condition, probably rheumatic fever. I was in bed for six weeks and was convalescent for a while. There were only a few weeks of my fifth and important term left when I did return to *Conway*. I had to do my fifth term again in the term that should have been my sixth. So when I left *Conway* I passed out at fifth term instead of sixth. This did not matter very much because I had officially completed my two years on a training ship. A years sea time towards my four year apprenticeship.

This fourteen to sixteen year age period was one in which the boys began to take an interest in girls. Some of the boat's crews were fine big fellows and Rock Ferry pontoon was reasonably secluded and free from people except when a ferry came in, but the service was not very frequent. There was a girl we called "Pontoon Cissy" who was a regular friend of the motor boat's crew. There were others, but "Cissy" was a regular and she even used to make a return trip to Liverpool on Sunday evening to meet the boys returning from Sunday leave. There were secluded places on the upper deck and the ferry would have few passengers, except the Conways.

Seniority was of tremendous importance in our lives. When you had to queue for anything such as getting the food from the galley for your mess, you pushed in behind the last of your term and ahead of anyone in the term junior to yours. So first termers were always at the end of the queue. Your pockets were sewn up until, I think, sixth term. Caps were always worn at divisions but at other times you were not allowed to wear your cap all day until 4th term. Looking back I realized that I almost lived in a uniform cap from that time until I left the Navy in 1946.

Looking back at it all and in spite of the parts which I did not enjoy, I realise what tremendous value those two years were to me. I had already been at a boarding school so being away from home did not worry me. I was never homesick, unless I was in some kind of strife and feeling sorry for myself. The boatwork and the discipline were beyond price. We learned to clean things. We cleaned the ship and cleaned the ship. We learned to scrub wood white. We learned to sweep so that not a speck of dust could be found in any corner anywhere. We learned to clean brass, not with the easy cleaners of today but with brickdust and oil and elbow grease. Brass had to be cleaned constantly. The sea air tarnished it almost as soon as it had been polished. We learned too to look after ourselves and our clothes. How to polish shoes. Simple things, I suppose, but how important a preparation for a boy on the verge of stepping out into the world. Men who have never had this sort of training - which is that of the armed services - are often helpless when faced with doing simple things for themselves. I have always been able to look after and care for myself. In later years have added cooking to my repertoire and which I enjoy.

I had always been inclined to chest troubles. Frequent colds and the climate in the Mersey was probably the worst that I could have experienced. Most of the year was cold and damp, and we were often wet from rain or from working in boats. The "Daily Mail" at this time used to carry full page advertisements for YADIL. This was supposed to be an extract of garlic and came in the form of pills, liquid, and I think a jelly. It was reputed to cure colds and chest trouble. I was then suffering from infected tonsils and my father who was also chesty was hooked on YADIL so it was sent for me to take too. I remember going to the sick bay three times a day for months for my YADIL It may have done me good, I don't know but garlic is good for the human body. When I went to sea and got some sun into me - my troubles disappeared and never returned. The conditions did me no harm and over those two years I grew some four inches and put on a lot of weight. I am still the same height I was when I left *Conway*.

During our last term and mine was the summer term of 1923 we began to think of our future. If we wished to continue with a sea career we had to go to sea in merchant ships as an apprentice. Or, one could start a part time naval career by joining the Royal Naval Reserve and doing some time as an R.N.R. Cadet and then midshipman. This latter course was closed to me as I had only done five terms and was not elegible to sit for the examination. After this the three year apprenticeship still had to be undertaken in order to put in the requisite sea time before sitting for a Second Mates Certificate. My letters of application had to be written to shipping companies of one's choosing We were quite familiar with the ships of many companies. They passed the *Conway* on their way up and down the Mersey. We were near enough to Cammel Lairds shipyard and we saw some of them launched. It was always an exciting time and those who could took up vantage points on the upper deck at high tide. A faint cheer was heard in the distance as the majestic hull of a new ship slowly started to move. Gathering speed she would enter the Mersey in a cloud of foam to be grabbed by the waiting tugs and taken to her fitting out berth.

There were still some big sailing ships in use in 1923 and I remember writing to the owners of one of them, the *Mount Stewart,* to apply for an apprenticeship. The reply was, however, that the ship had a full complement for her next voyage which coincided with my finishing on *Conway.* My only experience in sail had to remain at a couple of trips in a coastal ketch during a summer holiday. This ketch belonged to Aberayron and used to bring blue metal from a big quarry in an inlet about 36 hours sail from Aberayron. The crew consisted of the master and mate who doubled as engineer and myself (unpaid). We had a large hotbulb diesel engine for entering and leaving harbour. This engine took some time to start. First light the blow lamp to heat the bulb. When the bulb was red hot, lift the compression release and swing her over by hand - with a bit of luck, off we went.

After my failure to join a sailing ship I had to settle for steam and applied to Ellermans City and Hall Lines of Liverpool. I knew these ships well as I used to see them passing Conway on their way to the Manchster ship canal. The two lines were separate, but staff were interchangeable.

I no sooner arrived home at the end of the summer term of 1923 than a letter arrived from Ellermans Hall Line appointing me apprentice on the *SS. Croxteth Hall,* of 3132 tons register, with orders to join her in Liverpool where she was loading general cargo for South Africa.

My indentures which had already been signed showed that my father had to pay the Company the sum of £50 ($100) and that I would receive the princely salary of thirty shillings ($3) per month for the first year. £2 ten shillings ($5) for the second year and £4 ($8) for the third and final year. I was to receive full board on the ship and also laundry while in harbour. I did not need much more in the way of clothes - I already had my Conway uniforms. A new cap badge and overalls completed my sea going outfit. The story of *HMS Conway* and her 115 years history ending tragically in the Menai Strait will be found in Appendix 1.

Chapter 2

FAR AND WIDE
1923 and 1924

My recollection of joining the *Croxteth Hall* was one of rain and coal dust. The ship was in a dock at Birkenhead and had just finished loading bunker coal from a lighter; everything was filthy and I don't think I was too happy either. We sailed that night, my station was on the bridge with the 3rd officer, and headed down the Mersey. Our destination was Capetown. The ship was fully loaded with general cargo, everything from whisky to railway lines. I am a good sailor and though I felt a bit sick when we got out into the Atlantic swell, I soon got over it and have never been seasick since. This is a blessing as there are people at sea who suffer from chronic seasickness. The only saving for them is that there is much more fine weather sailing than bad weather sailing.

The ship was small, slow, and old. She had been built in 1909 at Bremerhaven as the "*Etha Rickmers*", and handed over to Britain in 1918 as part of the Great War reparations agreement. 365 feet long and 48 feet beam she had four holds, two forward of the engine room and two aft. The ships complement was Captain and three deck officers, 4 engineers, 2 cadets (apprentices), three white quartermasters, a white carpenter and an Indian crew. The deck Serang was the head of the seamen, the equivalent of a boatswain, and the engine room Serang was the head of the stokers and oilers. The officers' stewards and cooks were Goanese, from the Portuguese enclave of Goa in India. The crew had their own cooks. The engine room crew came from the Punjab and the seamen came from one of the ports, Bombay - Calcutta - Karachi - Madras. The sailors spoke a common language which is usually referred to as "lascari bat" or lascar talk and the men were referred to as lascars or lascar seamen. It was the only foreign language I ever actually spoke and used. It was very simple and could be used anywhere on the coast of India.

The ship burnt coal under her three marine type boilers, working at a pressure of 185 lbs square inch. Marine boilers are fire tube boilers where the fire goes through tubes to heat the water as opposed to water tube boilers used on land and in warships. In the latter case the water was in the tubes and the fire outside. The great difference was that the marine boiler was more trouble free but it took a great deal longer to raise steam. In a water tube boiler steam could be raised in an hour or so.

The engines had been built by Bremer Vulcan of Vegesack and were triple expansion steam engines of 327 nominal horse power. These engines were so called because the three cylinders were of different sizes. The high pressure cylinder was the smallest and the steam entered this one first, then the medium pressure in the middle and finally the low pressure - the largest. The sizes, in the case of the *Croxteth Hall*, were 23 1/2 inches, 38 1/2 inches and a quite massive 63 inches. The steam passed through the three cylinders and then passed to the condenser where it was turned back into water to be returned to the boilers. This created a vacuum in the exhaust side of the low pressure cylinder and gave some assistance to it. The propeller shaft ran through a tunnel through number 3 and 4 holds to drive a three bladed propeller at about 60 revolutions per minute. The two masts had derricks and winches to handle cargo. The hatches had wooden covers and these were covered with three or four heavy canvas tarpaulins, secured to the hatch combing with heavy iron bars dropped in behind cleats and wooden wedges between the cleats and the hatch bars. This method of securing hatches had lasted for many years, and during my years in merchant ships I only once saw a tarpaulin come free in an Atlantic gale. One of the carpenters duties was to go around hatch wedges with a heavy hammer to make sure they were tight at all times. The ships crew were responsible for covering and securing hatches when the ship was finished loading or discharging her cargo.

Apprentices, or Cadets as we were sometimes called, were supposed to be taught. We were, to the extent that we worked with the officers during their "watch" and took our own sights of the sun or stars to work out the ship's position. We were not actually taught by the officers but were shown how to do things the practical way. We ex-CONWAYS were fortunate in that we had been through all the navigation and seamanship, in theory, including ship construction and engineering. Which meant that all the teaching we needed was to be shown how to put our knowledge into practice. For practical seamanship we usually worked with one of the three white quartermasters. They taught us how to sew canvas, splice hemp and wire ropes and of course to paint. Chipping off rust and repainting was an everlasting job. In those days there were usually quite a lot of varnished doors, woodwork, rails, and the like. When it came to revarnishing chief officers demanded the woodwork be cleaned to the bare wood. Modern chemicals may make this easy but I am thinking of the days of sand and canvas, coconut husk, or bathbrick and sandpaper. This was the one job we really hated, though the finished product was beautiful as most of the woodwork was of teak. The Chief Officer was responsible for all the work of the ship, its cleanliness, discipline, repair and that the ship was in good condition and that everyone did their job. We did not work with the Indian crew. We were always either on our own, with an officer, or one of the quartermasters. It was usual for us to keep the four hour watches with an officer, and then do two hours in the morning or afternoon on deck work of some kind. Saturday and Sunday were days of no deckwork for us though the usual watches were kept. It was usual in ships where only two cadets were carried for the senior cadet to keep watch with the Chief officer 4-8 both am and pm, and the junior cadet to keep watch with the 3rd officer 8-12 also am and pm. The 2nd officer who kept the middle watch 12-4 was on his own. The arrangement worked very well, especially for the Chief officer who could leave the bridge in charge of his Senior Cadet (in open waters) and attend to the crew starting work for the day. They were both able to take their morning sun sights, which were important, as this gave longitudes for the ship's position. The sights at noon gave the latitude. From these two the noon position and day's run were worked out and any adjustment to the course could be made. Various people need to know the noon position, and it was usual for the forenoon watch cadet to take the chit, with the position and days run, to the Radio office and the Chief Engineer.

Things were simple in those days. Without modern electronics and satellite navigation aids, ships got round the world quite satisfactorily, though with perhaps more worry to the Captain when bad weather could make celestial navigation impossible for days on end.

Our voyage to Capetown was the opening of a new world to me. By the time we had reached the latitude of the Azores the sea had become smooth, with just a slight ocean swell and the sun was warm and bright. I had never seen the sun shine like this. Every day! And to feel warm and put on light clothes was all new to me, as I had never been out of the British Isles before. The miracle was that all my chest and throat trouble cleared up, never to return in a chronic form again. It took us 30 days to Capetown at a speed of 9 knots (9 nautical miles per hour) and the sight of my first foreign port was wonderful. One morning, towards the end of August 1923, I awoke to see Table Mountain with its white tablecloth of cloud and the town of

Capetown spread out below. Close by was Robben Island with its large gaol. Soon after we had picked up the pilot, we were entering harbour and we went to our stations. My place was on the bridge to keep a note of times, in a notebook, of the orders to the engine room. The Chief Officer was on the forecastle with the carpenter at the windlass, the Serang and some crew. The 2nd officer was aft, with his part of the crew, and the third officer was on the bridge and operated the engine room telegraph in response to orders from the Pilot or the Captain. Soon we were alongside the wharf in the harbour and I had my first sight of the black African dock labour force. We carried what was called general cargo. This consisted of all sorts of manufactured goods from Britain in boxes and bales, motor cars in boxes, and other machinery. I also remember a great deal of railway material, carriage wheels, springs and other parts, and railway lines.

We spent a few days in Capetown, my one and only visit. I don't remember going ashore, but I suppose that I must have done. Soon we were off to Algoa Bay and Port Elizabeth. At these two ports we discharged our cargo into lighters as there were no other port facilities. I do not remember going ashore there. The next port was East London, a small and pretty harbour protected by a breakwater and was, if I remember only walking distance from the town. Then on to Durban to discharge the last of our cargo. Durban I remember for the rickshaw pullers, huge black men dressed in very little but with a magnificent head dress of ostrich plumes. There was a beautiful bathing beach where we went for a swim. Large areas were protected by shark nets. Whites only were allowed to use this beach. Notices were everywhere in those days, reserving certain areas or facilities for whites. Durban was then known as one of the worst places in the world for sharks.

By now we had finished discharging all the cargo from Britain. Life at sea for a cadet on a merchant ship in those days was a fairly lonely one. There were two of us, but we were not always able to go ashore together. We had no money or very little. The sum of £1-10 per month, which we got during our first year at sea, did not go very far and we all smoked; even though a half-pound tin of cigarette tobacco only cost 5/-, we would still have had a small bill on board ship. So we had to rely on the quartermasters or officers for company. We were not encouraged to go ashore with the quartermasters - presumably in case they led us astray. The 3rd officer or a junior engineer would sometimes take us with them, and were just as likely to lead us astray, and probably did. Not much fun for a 16 year old. Various Missions to Seamen in the ports of the world did a marvellous job. They added somewhere to go and something to do to a cadet's day ashore in a foreign port. A reading room, billiard table, cheap cup of coffee, and the occasional dance run by the local ladies were usual. All was a little bare and spartan in those days, but we did not expect anything else. It was just good to get off the ship for a few hours and have somewhere to go. We seldom got to know local people in the ports we visited unless one already knew someone, or had an introduction. The exception to this were Australia, New Zealand, and North America. In the ports of these countries people went out of their way to meet us and look after us. Meeting families meant also meeting girls - a treat for lonely sailors.

Durban was left behind and our next port was Laurenzo Marques in Mozambique where we were to load coal. At that time Mozambique was Portuguese East Africa and here we saw a different kind of life; which up to now had definitely been British. The coal loading was simple but efficient. The trucks of coal were, one by one pushed into a revolving cage, hoisted sufficiently to be above the ship then turned upside down and the coal went down a chute into the hold. As each truck was emptied a cloud of coal dust enveloped the ship. It seeped in everywhere and it was some time before we got our cabins and the ship really clean.

Laurenzo Marques was a lovely old Portuguese town with a population all shades of colour between white and black. Bars of all kinds were only walking distance from the ship. Too handy in this case because when we went ashore I got thoroughly filled up, and had my first real drunken experience. However this did not bring any good resolutions and, I am sorry to say, it was not the last time it happened.

Soon we were off again - it only took a couple of days for a full load of coal. This time we headed for Sabang, a small island at the North end of Sumatra. It is not heard of today, but then, it was an important coaling station on the trade route between Suez and the East.

We were now on a typical tramp steamer's voyage and having washed off the coal dust settled down to a three week voyage to Sabang. Up to now the weather, since leaving Liverpool, had been near perfect but halfway to Sabang we ran into a gale. I was thrilled. To stand on the bridge and look up at a great green sea ahead, with a curling white top, and the ship heading down into the trough. How slowly she rose - up and up but not enough, the white top broke over the forecastle, the windlass disappeared under green water, which now poured onto the well deck, over the canvas hatch covers, to end up against the central deck house and up to the square ports of the saloon on the deck above. The ship's speed was eased so that she just had steerage way - not enough to make the seas we were taking over the bow do any damage. The gale was a North Easterly, and we were pushing directly into it. However, it did not last long and after a couple of days we were again in lovely warm Indian Ocean weather. I was not frightened then - just thrilled. As I became more experienced a healthy respect and fear of the sea developed. Later, in small ships on the China coast, with full responsibility for the safety of the ship and its crew, I shunned bad weather and took every opportunity to shelter. The power of the sea cannot be mastered by man, he can only do his best to go along with it.

Life in a tramp steamer had a glorious uncertainty to it. You knew your next port, or series of ports to load or unload, but after that it was a mystery. We signed on three year articles in Liverpool and the ship could stay away for that time if it suited the owners. It made correspondence with us difficult and we had to let our people know where to address us next - as soon as we knew. After Sabang we had no idea of where we were going to next. Always a source of speculation and conversation; but there were always some clues. We knew we would not go back to Africa empty. The possibility was that we would load another cargo somewhere not too far away - Singapore and Far East or even Australia. But where then, U.K. or U.S.A? Sabang at last. A beautiful land locked harbour set in the greenest of green islands. There was a coal wharf, with its unloading cranes, and huge piles of coal, and a small native village with some European houses further up the hill. All clean, tidy, very well kept and under Dutch control. Java and Sumatra were Dutch Colonies, which after 1946 became Indonesia. The unloading was slow as this was done with cranes and grabs and finished off by hand.

News had now come that we were to go to India and Ceylon and load a full cargo for the U.K. What joy. It was after all only going to be a six months voyage and everyone was pleased. Not home for Christmas but that did not matter. So with the unloading finished we were off to Goa where we loaded a parcel of manganese ore, and took the opportunity of changing our Indian crew. The stewards were in their home port but the others had been recruited in Bombay and were returned there. From Goa we loaded at small places along the Malabar Coast. With the exception of Cochin, where we went to a wharf, we loaded from lighters in the open sea. What a lovely scented cargo. Bales of coconut fibre, bales of coconut mats and matting. The scents came from bags of nutmegs, pepper, peanuts and other spices from this flourishing part of India,

Kerala State. One of a cadet's jobs was to watch the stowing of cargo, see that spaces were properly filled, and that there was no pilfering. One memory I have is of giving myself a stomach upset from eating too many peanuts from a broken bag.

Finally on to Ceylon and Colombo harbour where we topped off the cargo with chests of tea. Looking back on it all I seem to have enjoyed the new sights and sounds, the smell of the tropics, but was not terribly interested in the people or the places. I just accepted everything around me. I sometimes think of all the lost opportunities for seeing things of interest, but on the other hand there was not much chance. We seldom, if ever, got ashore during the day. There was work to do, and in any case money was always a problem. Another, was it the done thing? In my years at sea I never remember anyone who tried to combine tourism and seafaring.

We were off home and our next stop would be the Suez Canal. The Red Sea. The sea isn't red but everything else is, the cliffs, the sands, the sunrise and the sunset. Hot too, if you have a following wind, and the stokers come up on deck now and again for a breather. If no cool air comes down the large engine room ventilators, it can get pretty hot shovelling coal and raking hot ashes out of the furnaces. The various lighthouses in the Red Sea - how well I was to get to know them in the years to come. Suez, where we anchored to pick up the pilot; the huge searchlight which was hung over the bow to use at night in the canal. We also embarked a rowing boat and mooring crew. Two ships could not pass in the canal at that time. One of them had to tie up to the bank to let the other pass. There were special places for this with bollards set in the bank to tie up to. When we had to stop the boat was lowered over the side and the mooring ropes taken ashore. The other ship passed, the ropes were let go, the boat picked up and off we went until the next stop.

Then Port Said, where we moored to buoys and soon the ship was swarming with bumboat men, selling everything under the sun. Dirty pictures were always produced if one said no to everything else on offer. We were invited to go ashore - nice clean girl, very cheap and so on. I never went ashore in Port Said in the many times I passed through the canal. We filled up with coal and fresh water and sailed on into the Mediterranean. The sudden change in the climate always fascinated me. Port Said was hot, smelly, and sort of tropical. As soon as we left it became cool and fresh with a whole different feeling.

We stopped at Marseilles to discharge a small quantity of cargo and went ashore for a walk along the Rue Cannebiere and a few drinks. But we were all much more interested in getting home than exploring Marseilles. We soon passed out into the Atlantic where it was different again, with an ocean swell, it got progressively cooler each mile we went North. I remember the scent of the pines coming off the Spanish coast. We had not smelled pine scent for six months.

We were bound for London and now came my first trip through the English Channel where there were so many ships in sight at once. It was a busy time on the bridge - navigating and keeping a lookout for other ships. The Captain spent most of his time on or near the bridge, checking our navigation and watch keeping. The pilot met us at Dungenss, or thereabouts, and soon we were secure in one of the London docks. My first voyage was over. It was a never to be forgotten experience and one of much learning. I must have absorbed an incredible amount of new information in those few months. I had seen many places quite new to me. I had worked with men and managed to hold my own. I had seen the sea in many of its moods and it was just past my seventeenth birthday. Of the other cadet, there were two of us, I have no recollection. He would have been senior to me but he made no lasting impression. We must have got along together in a neutral sort of way. The other officers are gone from memory too, but I do know they were caring and interested in us youngsters. They passed on their knowledge in a simple way without actually teaching us. The things we never learnt on a school ship were beginning to find their place in our knowledge. I had been as happy as I ever remember; well treated, well fed, and on friendly terms with the officers, the engineers and the quartermasters.

When the Captain came back from his visit to Ellerman's London office he said I was to go home on leave and await instructions. So I packed my bags and set off to Paddington Station for the long train trip to my home at Aberayron. I had been paid up to date but had to pay my fare home. You didn't get much given to you and in those days there were no privileges, you had to fend for yourself.

I suppose we were exploited though at that time we did not look at it that way. When I needed extra money for something, such as fares or clothes, I had to appeal to my parents. Later, when I needed to be ashore for study and to pass my examinations for the various certificates, I had to appeal for help. You just had to save your money if your parents could not help. We did a lot of work on the ship which must have been worth something, and remember, my father had already paid £50 for me to become an indentured apprentice. Officers and crew got no overtime. If there was a job to be done - we did it. Saturday afternoon and Sunday were free, as long as the ship was quietly at sea, but we might be in port with all sorts of odd jobs requiring to be done. British seamen did get some overtime but it was usually frowned upon by the shipowner. Indian and Chinese crews did not get overtime.

Some ship owners would have one ship in their fleet set up as a cadet ship and would take as many as, say, 40 cadets to run the ship with a few seamen - mainly as instructors. These companies were able to employ most of those who applied for employment when they obtained their 2nd mates certificates. However, they did have a ship which did not cost much to run by way of crews wages.

The history of exploitation in the maritime industry goes back many years into the era of sail, where sailors were carried on board drunk and woke up to find themselves at sea bound for South America or Australia. Possibly the men who worked on the wharves were the worst off as the labour was casual. The men turned up for work and the foreman picked their gangs. The biggest and strongest usually got picked first and those that were not chosen had to come back and try again tomorrow. Today, where the men get attendance money, even if there is no work - things are naturally much better but there is a backlog of bitterness still evident between ship owners, stevedores, and their men. This always makes negotiation between the seamen's or wharf worker's unions very difficult, particularly in Australia where shipping charges are still too high and the workforce still too large.

It was wonderful to see Aberayron again. I was, I suppose a bit of a hero. Everyone wanted to know all about it. Though we were "foreigners" in Wales, people were very kind and caring and my parents had made friends in the little town. My father's particular interest was the river Aeron fishing board. He was a keen fisherman and had become a member of the board which was responsible for the river, which ran through the town. Nearly all the men of the town went to sea in one way or another. Most were deck or engineer officers and the others, there were not many, were seamen. From the colour the houses were painted, you could tell what company they belonged to. 'Funnel colour' paint made very good house paint, and it was suspected that it came home with the owner at the end of a voyage.

One lad from Aberayon had been on the *Conway* at the same time as I. He was older and a year ahead. He was one of the many Lewis'es and was nicknamed "Guffy". Can't say that I ever liked him. We used to compete for the favours of one of the local girls, so there was some reason. One of my great friends was the son of the local monumental mason. I would sit for hours and talk and watch him as he chipped the name of the deceased on a granite or marble slab. A rather morbid occupation, especially as he would have known most of the deceased, but one requiring great skill - one mishit and you ruined a beautiful piece of polished granite. Power tools were a thing of the future.

We used to wear uniform quite a lot in those days when on leave. I could not afford a lot of plain clothes as well as uniforms, so my uniforms became my good clothes. Maybe this was what attracted the girls. I knew most of the local girls and to "walk out" in the long summer evenings, usually with the same one was the thing to do. There was nothing else to do anyway. Occasionally there was a travelling picture show, and sometimes a dance in the hall. Both of these were few and far between.

It must have been about this time that I acquired my first motor bike. A variable gear, belt driven Enfield and my first driving licence - no examinations just a 5/- fee.

My father did not keep a car, though we had one in Ireland. Life was too exciting to be confined to a world bounded by the distance one could walk and cycling was not much fun either; so a motor bike was the answer. An Aunt and Uncle lived some miles away with two children a bit younger than I. I was fond of this family and a motor bike made it possible to go and see them whenever I felt like it. It is often easier to talk to uncles and aunts than ones own parents. I used to confide my troubles and listen to my Uncle, whereas his two children used to go to my father with their troubles. Especially the girl cousin who thought a great deal of my father who, I suppose, I never really appreciated. Parents have fixed opinions and my father used to say that no one should be given a driving licence unless they had driven horses on the road. Perhaps I see what he meant better today than I did then.

I was an only child, so home life was never much fun and I had to find my entertainment outside. However the motor bike gave me a marvellous new found freedom and I was able to go where and when I wanted, and with whom. My parents sometimes grumbled that they did not see much of me. My school years had all been spent at boarding schools and the *Conway;* now I was going to sea. I see their grumble was valid, but I did not think so then. One incident has stuck in my memory over the years and has made me realise how selfish and self centred one can be. I came home on one of my holidays and my father said various people had been asking after me, wanting to know when I would be home again. To this I said "Oh! What do they want to know for? My father quite rightly blew up and said "you ought to be damn glad that anyone takes that much interest in you." My first lesson that you have to be interested in other people as well as yourself.

When my first holiday from the sea came to an end a letter from Head Office in Liverpool arrived instructing me to join the *S.S. Merton Hall* in Manchester. This was to be my longest voyage.

Manchester was wet, drizzly and dirty - as usual, The ship was empty and ready to go to New York to load, what and for where - we did not know. The funnel looked a bit short to me and missing its black top and white band. The Ellerman City and Hall funnel was yellow with a black top and a white band in between. The explanation was, the funnel was too tall to go under the bridges over the Manchester Ship Canal and the top section had been unbolted and removed at the lock on entering the canal. The masts had been lowered too.

The *Merton Hall* was slightly bigger and older than my last ship. Her registered tonnage was

4988, with a length of 392 feet, and a 48 feet beam. She had been built by Swan Hunter and Wigham Richardson at Newcastle, in 1905. I do not remember the officers, except that the Captain's name was T. Cooper and it was his first command. The other cadet was senior to me. His name was Ian Macallam and he was very Scottish. Slightly different from the Croxteth Hall, the new ship had five holds. No 3 was a deep tank but did not have a dividing longitudinal bulkhead in the middle. Otherwise she was pretty much the same. Our cabin opened out onto the deck on the starboard side and was close to the ash hoist. So at the end of every watch we were woken by the rattle of the hoist, and the noise of the firemen shouting as they hoisted and dumped overboard the ashes from the boiler room.

As time went by, I grew to hate the Scottish cadet who was my cabin mate. He had gone straight to sea for a 4 year apprenticeship, our backgrounds were very different and he was a bit rough and difficult to understand We used to have quite savage fights in our cabin, and I remember one where I had got him on the floor and his sudden scream made me realise that his head was against a hot steam pipe leading to our cabin radiator. Fortunately he was not with us for long. After a few months he was transferred to another ship that had no cadets. We cadets were quite useful and were more help than hindrance on board.

There were many seamen's jobs we could do and yet did not have to work with the crew. When the time came for us to leave Manchester, I can remember a beautiful sunny day as we sailed past green fields on either side of the canal on our way to the river Mersey. People on the bridges waved to us as we passed. On arriving at the entrance lock of the canal the top black and white section of our funnel was standing on the wall waiting for us. It did not take long to lift it into place and bolt it down. When the lock gates opened we steamed out into the Mersey on what was the beginning of the longest and most exciting voyage of my whole time at sea in merchant ships. I have never seen the Manchester Ship Canal again, and I doubt if it is as much used today as it was 60 years ago, if at all.

I joined the ship on the 1st of January 1924 and we sailed a few days later. We were to face the North Atlantic in mid-winter, when it was always likely to be in a dangerous mood. This time it was. The voyage to New York was expected to take eleven or twelve days and we were sailing "in ballast". That is the holds were empty, all the double bottom tanks were full of sea water, and the bunkers full of coal.

Soon after we were clear of the North coast of Ireland we ran into a gale. The weather got colder and colder with snow squalls every now and again. I was keeping watch with the 3rd officer, that is 8-12 (am and pm). We kept our watch from the wing of the bridge - on the lee side. There was a certain amount of protection, but one had to be in the open as nothing could be seen through the wheelhouse windows.

The weather got steadily worse and the ship was more or less "hove to", and making practically no headway, even though we were heading in more or less the right direction, the gale being North Westerly. Huge seas towered above the bridge and forecastle. It was frightening looking up at the crests of these enormous green monsters. The bridge would have been 30 feet above the water and still all you could see was a great green wall blotting out the horizon and some of the sky. I had never seen a sea like this before but at this time only felt excited and secure in the strength of the ship. The ship being light rose to meet the seas easily then, after being poised poised on the top, for a time, plunged down the other side with a sickening slide. The stern came out of the water and the ship shuddered to the vibration of a racing propeller. The Engineer on watch would do his best to control this by shutting down steam to the engines when the propeller

S.S. Merton Hall, Ellermans Hall Line.
Name changed to CITY OF SALFORD in 1926.
Photo: National Maritime Museum, Greenwich, London.

was out of the water and opening up again when it was covered. A rather haphazard method but to some extent effective - but very hard on the engineer.

I had never realized how much spring there is in a seemingly rigid structure such as a ship until I noticed the wooden deck outside our cabin "working". When the ship was poised on the crest of a huge wave the two ends naturally sagged and when in a trough between the waves the middle sagged. I soon noticed water being squeezed in and out of the seams between the planks of the wooden deck as the ship worked.

The days dragged by. A miserably cold four hours on the bridge , wrapped up in all the clothes you could put on, until midnight followed by a far too short time being thrown about in your bunk. At least the cabin and bunk were warm. Meals were hazardous with the fiddles (a framework placed on the table dividing it up into small sections to prevent crockery sliding) on the table. It was a marvel how the cook and the stewards managed to produce good hot meals on time. Some days we saw the sun and managed to snatch a sight and check our position. Some days we never saw the sun at all.

One day I noticed a crack had appeared in the steel plating of the deckhouse where our cabin was situated. I mentioned this to the Chief Officer who seemed quite unconcerned. I guess he had other worries. About this time I began to realise that we were in danger, and though we might not break in half there were many other things that could happen, such as losing our propeller. For the first time I felt afraid of the sea.

We were making very little progress and at the end of about ten days we were still only half way across the Atlantic and steadily using up the coal. This made the ship lighter still and almost unmanageable. The pitching motion changed to a terrible corkscrew motion as the ship's head came off the wind and we wallowed in the troughs. For hours the quartermaster would have the wheel hard over in an effort to keep the ship nearly head on to the wind and sea. We were all getting heartily sick of it, and though no one said anything I do not think I was the only one who was beginning to be afraid.

The coal was getting lower and the ship lighter all the time. One day the Captain made the decision to put water in the number 3 hold. This hold did not have a permanent fore and aft bulkhead in the middle but did have the shaft tunnel running through it - this was about ten or twelve feet high. He did not want to fill the hold with water, just enough to keep the propeller a bit more in the water. So we put two hoses into the hold - one each side of the tunnel and turned the water on. Looking back on it I cannot understand how a man who had been at sea all his life, could have made such a decision. The only excuse could be that the fuel situation was a lot worse than we thought. We may have started out with only enough coal to get us to New York. Coal was probably much cheaper in U.S.A. than in Britain. As the hold started to fill some heavy planks came loose from the bottom together with the rubbish that was the remnant of many cargoes. Anyway, things went well for a while, even though the heavy planks were swishing from side to side making fearful bangs, first against the tunnel and then against the ship's side. We had just turned the hoses off with the water about half way, or less up, the tunnel wall when the ship took a violent roll to port and a whoosh of water went over the tunnel to the port side which was our leeward side. This was followed by another one and more water went over the tunnel. Now to add to its troubles the ship had a list to port.

The situation was now worse than before and the Chief Engineer was asked to pump out the port side of the hold. This seemed to be the right solution, but as soon as the pumps were started the inlets got blocked with the rubbish swilling about in the hold, and it was far too dangerous to send anyone down to try and clear the inlets. The water would have been four or five feet deep, with heavy planks swishing from side to side as the ship rolled. We were stuck with the situation. A list to port making the ship not only more uncomfortable, but more difficult to steer.

Fortunately, in about forty eight hours or so, the weather began to moderate and we were able to get back on our course for New York. When we began to near our destination and had to look for the Nantucket light vessel off the mouth of the Hudson River we ran into thick fog. So we crawled, with the monotonous sound of our fog horn, stopping when we heard another vessel, until its position was ascertained. After some hours the fog lifted and we spotted the light vessel. We arrived in New York twenty one days after leaving Liverpool and tied up at a wharf of the Vacuum Oil Company in New Jersey - glad to be alive. I had my 17th birthday in mid Atlantic in one of the worst gales of 1924. Over the years many ships have been lost in such conditions as ours. Looking back I think we were very lucky.

We learned that we were to load case oil for Australia. This was great news, it really meant new horizons for me, the Panama Canal, the Pacific Ocean, and then Australia, another country where hospitality was a legend among seafarers.

Since the introduction of petrol pumps and bulk handling of petroleum products, case oil has long disappeared into history. The product, petrol, kerosene, or lubricating oil, was packed in a white wooden case with the name of the product and the Company stamped on the sides. Once the product had been used the case and the two cans came in for many uses. Cut the top off the can fit a wire run through six inches of broom handle and you had a fine bucket. Flatten it out and you had a sheet for the roof or the side of a shed. The wooden box had many uses, for fruit picking, for firewood, or for furniture.

The longshoremen (wharfies) had their own methods of loading the ship. They rigged up their gear, using the ships derricks, with rope instead or wire. The ships wire was removed from the winches and the ropes were then used off the barrel at the end of the winch shaft - a much quicker way than using the winch with wire wound round the main barrel of the winch in the orthodox manner. But first the holds had to be got ready and the No 3 hold with the water in it had to be pumped out and cleaned.

New York of happy memories. New York of gracious and warm hospitality. New York in mid winter, steam rising from gratings in the sidewalk. New York of a glass of milk and a piece of pie, or a stack of wheats and maple syrup. We were to spend quite a few days in New York while all this was going on. The first delight, I think was the lunch wagon that came to the wharf every day. By the time we got to New York we were heartily sick of the food. There was no refrigeration, and the large ice box kept on deck had long since been emptied and cleaned. Our joy was to go to the wagon for a piece of pie, usually apple, of generous proportions and a glass of milk. The fresh milk was delicious, and something we never saw on the ship.

A message came to every British ship on arrival at New York inviting any apprentices on board to visit the British Apprentices' Club. I believe it was on 23rd Street near 7th Avenue. Quite a way from New Jersey, but travel was the cheapest item we came across. On the subway you put a nickel (5 cents) in the turnstile and then you could go anywhere on the system. The elevated railway or "L" as it was called was the same. I think the trams were 8 cents and the same 'go anywhere system operated'.

The British Apprentices Club was really a home from home. It was run by a group of dedicated well-to-do American ladies, most of whom had some connection with Britain, who were using their money for the benefit of young Britons who would have been at a very loose end in New York. The exchange rate was about three dollars to the pound and our thirty shillings a month did not go far. These ladies organised trips to their homes and ran dances and other entertainments in the club. Coffee and sandwiches were always available and magazines and writing materials provided. If any lady who had anything to do with the BAC of New York or her descendants read this, please accept the author's deep gratitude for the care and friendship they extended to me.

There was of course the occasional visit to a cinema or a meal in one of the many restaurant chains. We discovered the delights of waffles or "a stack of wheats" (wheatcakes) with maple syrup. These were probably the cheapest items on the menu. We did not get ashore very much. The ship was loading up to 10 pm every night and I was always on duty with the 3rd officer. When we ran out of money we just stayed on board.

At last the loading was over, the ropes removed from the derricks, and our own gear restored. Hatch covers were put on and secured by our crew and we were ready to cast off. Leaving New York and heading South we soon ran into fine weather, which was to stay with us for many days to come. I realise now that fine weather is the usual at sea, and that gales and bad weather are just incidents to be put up with and left behind.

We were sitting on a fairly explosive cargo in a very ordinary old ship. The cargo now consisted of some 10,000 tons of petrol and kerosene in 5 gallon tins (U.S.gallons). Some of the tins leaked slowly - there was always a slight smell of kerosene or petrol until we got used to it. The petrol was stowed in the two holds furthest from the boilers and the kerosene and lubricating oil in number 2 and 3 holds nearest the boiler-room. Our bunker coal was stowed in the large cross bunker which was in fact just another hold between no. 2 hold with kerosene and the boiler-room. Coal was also stowed in the 'tween deck', under the accommodation either side of the ship. As the coal in the cross bunker was used and space became available, the firemen trimmed the between deck coal to an opening in the 'tween deck', where it fell into the cross bunker. This kept the cross bunker more or less full until such time as the 'tween deck' bunker was empty. This meant the oldest coal in the ship was that lying up against the forward watertight bulkhead of the cross bunker, on the other side of which was stowed cases and cases of kerosene. Here lay a sleeping dragon. Coal is subject to spontaneous combustion. The longer it lies in a heap, and undisturbed, the more likely it is that at some point it will start to burn by itself.

It was glorious weather all the way to the Panama Canal. After the cold of New York and the perils of the Atlantic this was the sort of weather that, to use our expression, "we felt we were paid for".

We anchored at Panama for a few hours to top up with coal and then made our way through the canal. The first experience of this canal is unforgettable; the deep green of the tropical vegetation, the great locks the ships have to go through at either end, and the locomotives that hauled the ship into the lock and held it there until the lock was filled or emptied. So unlike the canal at Suez.

The Pacific Ocean is a few feet higher than the Atlantic and, though you go up three locks, you only go down two at the other end. It was not long before we were in the Pacific Ocean, heading for Australia. Everyone looked forward to Australia - a land of legend. We were told it was a land where "the women have no virtue, the birds no song, and the flowers stink". Still we were eager to go, and as I was later to find out the saying was only partly true!!. Many years later I have come to love it as my adopted land. But that is very much later and another story altogether.

The Pacific, when in repose, is without doubt the worlds most beautiful ocean. We were crossing the calm part from Panama to Cairns in North Queensland. The North Pacific between Canada and Japan can be as rough and cold as the North Atlantic. The South, from New Zealand to Cape Horn is, as the name implies - the "roaring forties" 40° South Latitude).

The first land we saw were the Marquesa Islands, just green and tropical islands in the distance. In sight for a couple of hours or more and then left far behind. Of the thousands of islands I have seen from a ship somehow this one has stuck in my memory. I still have the photograph I took at that time.

Then to Pitcairn. At the Panama Canal we had been given a bag of mail and our Captain had promised to deliver it when we passed the island. Pitcairn was chosen by the mutineers of *HMS BOUNTY* because it was so isolated. It seemed unlikely they would ever be discovered by the Royal Navy, whom they knew might one day search for them. This isolation has persisted and the small self sufficient settlement is entirely dependant on passing ships for mail and goods. We approached the South side of the island, blowing our whistle, and soon two long boats were launched from a tiny beach and quickly rowed out to us. We handed over the mail and were given fresh vegetables in return. I believe they had souvenirs to sell but I don't think we had the time to spend bartering.

It was about this time during the voyage that the Chief Engineer came one day to the Captain and said that the temperature in the cross bunker was rising rapidly, and he thought the coal was probably on fire. The Chief Officer was sent for and plans were discussed to cope with the situation. The situation was not pleasant. The seat of the fire - if there was one - would be deep down in the many tons of coal filling the cross bunker. In the hold next to it were thousands of cases of cans of kerosene, some of which by now had started to weep or leak. Not many but enough to have a good layer of heavy gas in the hold.

The first thing to do was to locate the seat of the fire, which by now could by smelt as the fumes came up the ventilators. We were in fact a time bomb waiting to explode, though at times like this one does not seem to think of the dangers. The important thing was to find the fire and make sure air did not get to it; in which case it could easily become impossible to quench it with the ship's resources.

So we set to and started to move the coal back into the 'tween deck' bunkers, which were now empty, and get as much of it as possible out on to the stokehold plates - though there was not much room for this. We swung out the four lifeboats and made sure all the equipment was intact. We all set to, to shovel coal, ourselves, the crew, and off-watch firemen (stokers). Hoses were played on the coal and we hoped for the best!.

By now the smell of smouldering coal was almost overpowering and men could only work in the bunker for a short while. For some reason the Chief Officer took my mate and I off the work. We had just begun to enjoy ourselves - covered in sweat and coal dust and aspiring to be heroes. We were probably more use elsewhere and we were, I suppose, a certain responsibility to him. If anything happened to us it could mean deep trouble for the company.

After about three days of panic the temperature in the coal started to drop. The water we had pumped into the bunker had done its work and for the time being the fire was out. All that remained was to clean up the mess and keep a good watch on the temperature in case it started all over again. Fortunately the weather all through had been perfect. In fact the whole trip had been blessed with some of the most beautiful weather that I ever remember.

On arrival at Cairns we picked up the pilot and were taken to our berth alongside a wharf in the river. Wharves on one side and mangroves on the other, Cairns in 1924 was a sleepy place. With small weatherboard houses, set in tree lined streets, it was green, lush, and pretty in its way. It was hot, just after mid summer, and we wore our white uniforms with long trousers (no shorts in those days), when not doing dirty work. We were intrigued to see that the men working on the wharves were happy in thick heavy clothing: dark serge trousers, grey flannel shirts, and hats. It is odd what impresses one, but this is an impression that has remained with me always. We were quite close to the town; a little upstream from where the Marlin Jetty stands today, close enough for people to walk down to see a ship that had just come in.

After the hatch covers were taken off the unloading began. It was a slow process. Completely different from the speedy loading in New Jersey. Large canvas ventilators were hoisted over the holds and work started. We had some trouble with the petrol holds as the men kept complaining of gas. Each time this happened work stopped and the men working in the holds came up for a breather.

One day we were told that there was a crocodile under the wharf and asked if we had a pistol on board. The third officer got the pistol from the Captain and climbed down under the wharf to look for the crocodile. However during the search he somehow fell into the water and was rescued thoroughly frightened. That finished our valiant third officer for crocodile hunting and the wharfies had a good laugh.

We did not see much of Cairns. As usual a walk to the nearest pub was as far as we got. The cargo being for all ports to Melbourne meant only about 2,000 tons for each port. Cairns is inside the Great Barrier Reef, the largest coral reef in the world and the reef and the area enclosed are now a Marine National Park. In those days National Parks were a thing of the future. Although there is plenty of deep water for ocean going ships inside the reef, some of the navigation is a bit tricky, so we had to take a pilot to guide us to our next port - Townsville.

What is today a thriving town was in those days even more sleepy than Cairns. I remember going ashore one evening for a walk and not meeting a soul. Then it was on to Brisbane where we were allocated a berth at the Pinkemba wharf. The trip South from Cairns had been quite uneventful. We zig zagged through a series of pretty green islands with little white beaches. They all looked the same except the ones that had a lighthouse. There was no indication of the lovely holiday resorts some of them would become in the next 50 years or so. Certainly no one thought of the reef.

I don't remember going ashore at all in Brisbane. I was not to see it again till 55 years later when on a caravan tour of Queensland.

After Brisbane our next stop was Sydney and we berthed at a wharf at Pyrmont for what must have been quite a few days. The cargo was getting fairly well down in the holds by now and gas from the cargo was quite a problem to the men working in the holds. Sydney without "The Bridge"!. It is hard to imagine what it was like, then, but the ferries were fast and efficient. We visited Taronga Park Zoo; one of the largest and most efficient Zoos in the Southern hemisphere. We walked in the domain. Drank a lot of Australian beer; beer drinking seemed to be an Australian hobby. The men working the cargo had one of their number on the run to a pub, which was quite close, to bring back billy cans of draught beer. This saved them from being spotted drinking from a bottle. By the end of the day some of them were quite 'nicely-thank-you', and ready for a 'knock off' session at the pub, which in any case closed at 6 pm. I do not remember this happening in any other part of the world.

It was about this time I lost my fellow apprentice. This was no real loss to either of us as we disliked each other intensely. He was transferred to another of our company's ships and I was on my own. This suited me nicely. Being alone I was more acceptable to the Officers and the Quartermasters. We lost a quartermaster through illness about this time and I was put on as a replacement. This meant that whilst at sea I steered the ship for two hours, and then had four hours off. It took a bit of getting used to I might add. The midnight to 2 am watch was worst of all. Standing at the wheel, watching a compass in the middle of the night, it was hard to keep awake and one tended to drift off to sleep. One would wake with a start to find the ships head 10 degrees or more off course, then a little wheel in the right direction to bring her on course again, slowly, before the Officer of the Watch noticed it. Sometimes one was startled by a shout from the wing of the bridge, "Watch your steering quartermaster!!". On fine calm nights the ships wake could be seen stretching out behind. Any wiggles were only too obvious.

We finished discharging our cargo in Melbourne and were taken to an anchorage off Williamstown to await orders. However, we had a look at Melbourne while we were berthed at the wharf. I don't remember much about it except St Kilda and Luna Park. It was in the days of cable trams. Much is made today of the short line of cable trams in San Francisco. But Melbourne in the 1920's had some miles of cable tramways. Narrow tram cars, open at the sides and the passengers sat on hard wooden seats facing outwards on each side. The driver controlled the tram by his brake and a very large lever which, when he pulled on it, clamped the car to the moving cable under the roadway. It is a pity that Melbourne could not have kept some of those unique cable trams - the only place in the world where I ever saw them. Except, many years later, the special tourist trams in San Francisco.

The couple of weeks we spent at anchor off Williamstown were dull. We were too far away to get ashore so we did a lot of work on the ship and put the lifeboats in the water. This was a job that there was not often an opportunity to get done. The wooden lifeboats of that day needed to be put in the water as often as possible.

News came at last that we were to load wheat for Beira on the East Coast of Africa, starting at Adelaide. Very soon we were at Port Adelaide with a train alongside loaded with bags of wheat. Work was hard in those days before the general introduction of bulk handling of commodities. A bag of wheat weighed 180 lbs, which is about as much as a man can carry on his back. The bags were lifted off the rail truck, where two men worked pulling the bags to the door. They were placed on to the shoulders of another who carried them a few yards to the edge of the wharf. Five or six bags in a sling were then hoisted on board with the ship's gear, and lowered into the hold, and carried out to the corners and sides. A big gang of men were employed at each hold and they kept at it all day. It was the responsibility of the ship's officers to see that bags of wheat were well distributed in the hold. Spaces left between the bags and the ships side could cause the cargo to shift in bad weather. Wheat, even in bags, shifts easily. Loose it runs like water, and ships have been lost over the years through the shifting of a wheat cargo.

From Adelaide we went to Wallaroo in the Spencer Gulf. In those days nothing but a jetty, a huge pile of bags of wheat, and a small village with a hall. It must have been a weekend because we were all invited to a dance at the hall. Everyone was pleased to see a ship and we really felt that we were welcome. But we were soon on our way again across the Great Australian Bight to Fremantle.

I was sorry to leave Adelaide because there I met my first Australian girl. Her name was Dorelle. She and a friend had wandered down to the wharf looking at the ships and we had asked them on board. She lived close to the port and her father worked in the cold store. In a couple of days we had established a sound friendship and I had even been asked to tea to meet her family. I did not know it then, but I was to see her quite a few times more.

Fremantle was our next port of call and here we finished loading the wheat cargo. As the holds became full, a number of bags in each layer were "bled". In other words they were slit with a knife and the wheat allowed to escape. This had the effect of filling the spaces between the bags to lessen the danger of movement. I must have run out of money by the time we got to Fremantle because I do not remember going ashore there. In any case the view from the bridge of the town was quite depressing - there seemed to be acres of rusty tin roofs. One wondered whether there could be anything of interest under them.

The voyage to Beira took us exactly 28 days and the weather was fine. Instead of going by the shortest Great Circle Course, which would have taken us into the bad weather of the Forties and head winds, we took a straighter but longer one and kept in the fine weather latitudes.

Of Beira, I have no recollection except that we were there for some days getting rid of the wheat. Then it was to Lorenzo Marques for a load of coal. The same voyage as we had made in the *Croxteth Hall*. But this time we had sad news in store when we got to Sabang. There was a message for us, from Liverpool, saying that we were to load in Singapore and Java for New York, instead of going home, as we hoped. So it was to be turn left at Gibraltar instead of turn right for the English Channel.

New York again and the British Apprentices Club. It was summer this time, or at least the weather was warm, and we were to discharge our cargo and load general cargo for South Africa. Being summer, straw hats were very much the fashion. They were straw "boaters" with coloured bands. Wearing our straw hats we thought we looked very American. However disillusionment came when two of us went into a cafe and sat down. The waiter came over and after looking at us asked "Ham and eggs, chief?" Obviously we were not as American looking as we thought.

The discharging and loading again took some time. We were to load general cargo this time and not case oil. The Captain gave me a long weekend leave so that I could visit an American friend of my Mother's who lived in Philadelphia. A lecturer, she taught at Bryn Mawr College, a women's university college of world repute. This was my first opportunity to go outside the port of the many places we had visited. I was impressed by the bustle of Grand Central Station and the fast trip in an express train to Philadelphia.

My one vivid recollection of the visit was a motor car trip to see the battlefields where the British were defeated in the War of Independence. The obvious choice of how to entertain a visiting Britisher. I remember rolling green lawns, memorials to the fallen, old canons, and other relics. This lady, whose name was Olga, and her friends, really went out of their way to entertain me with the finest of American hospitality. But soon it was all over and I had to get back to the ship for the next leg of our voyage.

After discharging our cargo in South Africa it was a load of coal again, this time for Bombay. At Bombay we discharged into lighters, a bit primitive in those days, mostly unloaded by women with little baskets. I don't think we went ashore. We were anchored out and the work went on night and day so that it did not take too long, but was very unpleasant. Then we learnt we were to pick up a cargo at Colombo and Malaya for Australia. Joyful tidings indeed. If we could not go home Australia was the next best place.

At Fremantle we learnt that we were to do a number of trips round the Australian coast to Sydney and back to Java, Singapore, and Penang. However after our first trip they cut out Sydney leaving us with Fremantle, Adelaide and Melbourne, We did not expect to be very long in any of the places but it also meant a week or ten days at sea at a time was all we would do. It was the long 28 or 30 day drags that are so monotonous. The icebox became empty after a couple of weeks and the food became very uninteresting. Adelaide was the port I was looking forward to and Dorelle had been writing to me quite regularly.

When we got to Melbourne, to finish discharging the cargo from Malaya, I was contacted by an Aberayron man called Tom Parry. He was older than I but I had met him a number of times in Wales. That evening he took me to a party at the home of friends of his. Tom was on an Australian coastal ship and I think the house belonged to one of his seaman friends It was a good party, though most of them were a little older than I. There was plenty of beer and we rolled up the carpets and danced to the gramophone. As the evening came to an end and the others were leaving our hostess said to me "you don't need to go yet". We had a cup of coffee, and then much to my surprise, she suggested I stay the night. She said I would have to be up early before her children woke up. By this time I must have been about 19, but very inexperienced, and this was certainly a new experience for me. I hope she was not too disappointed in me. I never found out what the motive was and I can only think she must have been pretty lonely. In later years I have learnt that at that period, and up to the post war years, Australian husbands did not take much interest in their women folk. Men would go for holidays together and leave the women at home. At parties the men would congregate round the beer keg and the women were left to talk among themselves. So perhaps a nicely spoken lad from England was a welcome stranger. She woke me early and I slipped out of the glass doors onto the veranda. I was told to put my shoes on at the edge of the veranda. All was well, the kids didn't wake, and I got a taxi back to the ship. I never met Tom again or his friends.

This incident was quite unusual. Attitudes to sex, seventy years ago, were very different from what they are today. Penalties for infidelity were harsh and it was long before the introduction of 'no fault' divorce. My subsequent encounters with girls were much more of an ordinary 'boy meets girl' nature. Sex before marriage was not acceptable for a number of reasons and almost no young woman would be prepared to 'go all the way' unless there had been a firm promise of marriage. Should the engagement fail, the young man would find himself in court, being sued for 'broken promise'.

We did not go to Melbourne again. It was decided that the trip from Penang to Melbourne via Fremantle and Adelaide made the time between voyages too long and in future our turn round point was Adelaide. This suited me very well, it meant that I was to get a few days with Dorelle at the end of each voyage.

Other things were now catching up with me. Time had rolled on to July 1926, we had been away from home for 2 1/2 years. I had worn out the clothes I came away with. I appealed to my father who sent me 10 pounds, quite a sum in those days. I bought some of the things I needed, though the quality seemed to me much poorer in Australia than what I would have got at home. The big thing for me was I had come to the end of my three years apprenticeship. I had thoroughly enjoyed it except for the first few months with my incompatible cabin mate. It was now time to work toward my examinations and move up in the world.

I had a brilliant idea now that my indentures had expired. We were in Adelaide and I suggested to the Captain that I be paid off and sit for the examination for my 2nd mate's certificate in Australia. The idea being that I could then get a job on the Australian coast and, I hoped, on a ship that called at Adelaide. There was much more coastal shipping in those days than there is now. Road and rail transport has killed the transport of goods between coast ports by sea.

The Captain was very good and did not knock back the suggestion right away - not that he had the power. My agreement with the company had expired and I could not be kept against my will. He made inquiries ashore and came back with a very sanguine report. If I got my ticket in Australia I would have to join the Merchant Service Guild before I could get a job. The Guild had closed its books as members were unemployed. It was a case of no guild membership, no job. I accepted his advice that my idea was not a good one, but because of Dorelle I was sorry to give it up. He must have cabled Liverpool because the next day a telegram arrived saying that I was to transfer to the *CITY OF WINCHESTER,* another of the Company's ships, that was in Adelaide at that time loading frozen meat for the United Kingdom. So ended another chapter in my career. By now I was a big lad of nineteen with three years sea experience and two years of training in *HMS Conway* behind me.

Chapter 3

THE ROAD HOME
1926

The *City of Winchester* was very different from the previous two ships I had served in. First of all she was comparatively new. She had been built in 1917 so was only nine years old. Her registered tonnage was 7981, about twice the size of *Croxteth Hall*. She was driven by two steam turbines coupled to one shaft, and designed to burn oil fuel or coal. All her holds were refrigerated. Built by Palmers & Co of Newcastle she was 456 feet long and 58 feet beam. In fact it was the largest ship I ever served in.

I transferred to her in Adelaide, where she was loading frozen beef for the U.K. There were no apprentices so I was to find myself in the position of a sort of 4th Officer. Unpaid of course, as my indentures clearly stated that I would remain on the apprentices' rate of pay until I could be returned home. The new position was good experience. I was supposed to be responsible, though I do not think I really was. When it came to watch keeping I was detailed to keep the 4-8 watch with the Chief Officer. This meant I was left in charge of the bridge during daylight hours, provided we were in open water; the Chief Officer kept on or near the bridge during the few hours of dark there was during his watch. I don't remember his name, but we got on well together and he helped me with my work as much as he could. I took morning and evening sun and star sights to check the ship's position. A great help with my exams later.

The operation of a refrigerated ship was different from what I had got used to. The main difference was that we had extra Engineer Officers. Their job was to look after the refrigerating machinery and make sure all the holds were kept at the proper temperature so the cargo arrived in tip-top condition, On the outward voyage they had an easy time and only had to ensure that the machinery was overhauled and ready for use when needed.

An oil burning turbine ship was quite a novelty. There was no rattle and bang of ash hoists every four hours as the stokers dumped overboard the ashes accumulated during their watch. The deep hum of the turbine at sea was a quite different sound from the thump thump of a large reciprocating engine. All in all she was a very pleasant ship to sail in, nice and clean with a very clean cargo.

We left Adelaide and called at Launceston and Hobart to load more frozen meat. We were not long in either place but in Launceston someone took me out to an apple orchard and I had a ride on an enormous motor bike. It was a twin cylinder "Indian", an American machine, painted red with the picture of an Indian Chief on the tank. A make which quietly disappeared. I have not even seen one among the veteran car and motor cycle exhibitions.

In Hobart we tied up at a wharf quite close to the IXL Jam Factory. At lunch time and again at knocking off time there would be a parade of girls past the ship. Some paused to chat with us hoping to be asked on board. You could always tell the girls who worked in the jam factory as their hands were stained with fruit juice.

Our next port of call was Auckland, a few days across the Tasman Sea. What a pretty place it was in those days, and I am sure it still is. There is a greenness about New Zealand, missing in Australia. The houses are similar or rather were similar; single story with red iron rooves and surrounded by trees. There were tree lined streets and pubs that closed at six p.m. in those days.

Because I was on my own, I did not have to stay on board and keep ship after work had finished. This was done by the 2nd and 3rd Officers. So I was able to go ashore every night. By day we loaded carcases of frozen lamb, a slow job as great care had to be taken not to bruise the meat. The dock labour was very partial to kidneys and it was part of our duty to watch the cargo being stowed in the holds. A quick slash of a knife would open the muslin cover on the carcase and another quick slash would remove a pair of frozen lamb kidneys. Easily stowed in a coat pocket of the heavy clothing worn for work, kidneys could make a welcome addition to a wharf lumper's breakfast. The unfortunate part of this was the carcase would be rejected for human consumption in the U.K. Kidneys had to be intact and attached to the carcase when inspected.

It was cold work watching cargo being loaded in a refrigerated hold. The men working kept moving all the time, stowing the cargo as it came down from the wharf, but the Officer watching just had to stand and watch. There were constant arguments between the wharfies and the engineers. The latter were responsible for the temperature in the hold, and the men refused to work if they felt the hold was too cold. The Union had a rule that men could not work below a certain temperature. Work proceeded slowly, with periods when everyone came up from below because it was too cold; or would not go down after lunch for the same reason.

We did not mind how slow the work went. I expect the Captain worried about it, but everyone else was pleased. New Zealand was filled with friendly people who spoke one's own language and welcomed ships from Britain and those who sailed in them.

It was a Sunday when we arrived in Auckland. In the afternoon two girls wandered along the wharf. The third officer and myself went down to talk to them. "Would you like to come on board and look round?" I asked. "Oh, we would like that", replied the youngest one. She was tall and pretty with long fair hair. She said her name was Esme and the family were Scandinavian, their name was Sorensen. The elder girl, Jane, demurred. "I don't think we really have time, I have to out tonight". "Just a few minutes pleaded Esme, "I love the smell of ships". We showed them round, the ship was clean and tidy, having just come infrom sea.

While out of earshot of the others; I said to Esme " Would you like to come to a movie tonight?" "There are no movies in Auckland on Sunday but you could come to our flat for the evening meal, Jane will be out". She gave me the address and soon after they wen ashore.

"I'm so glad you came. I was afraid you might have found something better to do" was her greeting when she opened the door of her flat. "Sounds as if you don't trust sailors", to which she replied "Well, would you?". She was probably right. Esme fed me well and we had a couple of nice cold beers. I did not stay too long and was careful not to do anything to frighten her. "May I see you again tomorrow, I have work during the day until the wharfies knock off. I do not have to stay board in the evening". "Do that" she replied "we could go dancing".

It was late when I was able to clean up and get off ashore. My trouble was that I had little or no money and I hoped the dancing would not be expensive. However all was well. Esme seemed to be pretty flush and paid our entrance to the dance all and for a soft drink, then back to her flat for some beer. Two things Esme liked were dancing - she was a good dancer - and beer which suited me too.

We spent most of the week in Auckland and each evening I spent with Esme. I was getting quite fond of her and though we never went far, she always enjoyed a good cuddle and roll on the sofa. Esme told me that an uncle of hers had a sheep station in the North Island. She suggested that if I could get paid off the ship, I was assured of a job on her uncle's sheep station.

I saw no prospect of the Captain, who had been instructed to return me to Britain, agreeing to this.

So on our last evening in port, I decided to jump ship. We had been out dancing as usual. Then a couple of beers in Esme's flat, so it was fairly late when I went back to the ship to get my gear. I got to my cabin and put a few things in my suitcase. By this time I felt a bit tired so lay on my bunk for a ten minute snooze.

I woke with a start as someone banged on my cabin door. It was the duty Quartermaster to tell me that we were to sail in half and hour and the pilot was on board. As I stood at my place on the bridge and waved goodbye to pretty Auckland, I thought there would be one young woman who must have wondered what happened to me. I have had a lot of luck in my time: this was one of the greatest pieces of luck I can remeber. Not onlt, would I have broken the law by jumping a ship on which I had 'signed on' in Adelaide, I was also goning to land in New Zealand as an illegal immigrant. Of course you never think of those things at the time. The growing up process proceeds, but sometimes it goes a bit slowly.

We were off down the coast to Wellington and after Wellington to Omaru in the South Island. This small coastal port served a rich hinterland. The Canterbury plains are known all over the world for the quality of lamb produced there. I used to think that Canterbury lamb came from England. It was not until I learned about the Canterbury Plains, while at Omaru, that I realized it was the best New Zealand lamb.

Work in Omaru proceeded very slowly. We waited for meat to come down to the wharf in rail trucks; we waited for the wharfies to decide if the holds were not too cold to work in. We waited for the rain to stop. No one minded a good spell in a nice little port. The day after we arrived there was a dance in the Omaru hall and all who could went along. It was good fun and everyone was very friendly. After all we were the only ship in port. I had a number of dances with an attractive girl who danced very well. She apologised because she was so lame. Interestingly, it did not seem to interfere at all with her dancing but was noticeable when she walked. She allowed me to walk home with her after the dance and I was to see her again. The next time we met she asked me if I played bridge. On hearing we played a lot of bridge on the ship, 'Auction' in those days, she invited me to tea (evening meal).I duly presented myself at 6.00 p.m. the next day. After the meal two men came in, much older than I, and friends of her father. I had expected that it was just going to be "fun" bridge with the family but it turned into a men's four - three men and one boy. "Is a shilling a hundred all right? I was asked. I acquiesced readily without realising it could be expensive - we usually played penny bridge on the ship (a penny a 100). Away we went and played steadily for a while. By the time we were getting to the end of the evening I realized I was about 30 shillings down and I don't suppose I had more than 10 or 15 shillings in my pockets. However my luck suddenly seemed to change and by the end of the evening I was only about two shillings down. I realized later that they had been kind to me. Not wishing to take money from a lad off a ship, they made it easy for me and my partner to win.

Dunedin was our next and last port of call. We were not there for long and by now we had a full cargo, nearly all lamb except for some beef loaded in Australia. Dunedin was the only place in the world I came across male prostitutes touting for business. Mincing along with flaunting handkerchiefs they accosted us, as presumably we looked as if we might mean business. It was odd that in those days, in such an isolated place as Dunedin, there would be homosexual men touting for business.

We were to return home via Cape Horn and call in at Buenos Aires for fuel. The Southern

Ocean was as cold and windy as ever. We rolled along, wind behind us, deeply laden and on the Great Circle course which took us well to the South. Beautiful albatross with their huge wing spread followed the ship for days, staying in the air for hours at a time with barely a movement of their wings. Superstitious sailors would never kill an albatross, it was sure to bring very bad luck. Today the bird is killed in hundreds by the hooks of long line fishermen.

I am glad to say that I have been round Cape Horn. It was summer, and the weather was cold, with a strong Westerly wind. But for me Cape Horn was just land on the horizon, as the Captain gave it a wide berth and did not try to go through one of the channels which offered a short cut.

Soon it was warm weather again and a day in Buenos Aires to fill up with oil fuel was our only stop before arriving in London. There is a tremendous thrill in arriving home after a long voyage. The climate seems to change, the sea changes from blue to green and everyone gets 'channel fever'. Quarrels and feelings between members of the crew are all forgotten. The last bit of paintwork has been touched up by the crew. It was usual to paint the ship on the way home so everything looked smart on arrival for the inspection of the Company's Marine Superintendent. We docked in one of the enclosed London Docks. In no time I was in a train for Aberayron. I had completed my apprenticeship. At last I had finished the sea time required before I could sit for the Board of Trade Certificate as 2nd mate.

Now I was free to do as I wanted. No more was I tied to a shipping company and if I wished, I could leave the sea forever and try for something else. I do not think that thought occurred to me then. It was not until later, when I began to fall in love, that the urge to leave the sea came upon me.

It was wonderful to be back in Aberayron again after 2 1/2 years, and to see my parents and friends. The monumental mason's son, still chipping names into slabs of polished granite, had hardly been out of Cardiganshire. I had been around the world a couple of times and seen many places.

I have no regrets for my time in merchant ships. In later life it quite cured me of ever being a tourist. I feel I know what almost every country in the world is like. Passenger ships, as such, are no more and one has to travel by air. Somehow travel does not seem travel to me when one drops in from the sky, takes off in an hour, and continues on ones merry way to a destination. Admittedly there are still plenty of cruise ships where life on board is organised to the limit. But it is not the same thing.

One is reminded of the story of the two young women who met after their holiday and whose conversation went like this:

"Hello" says first girl "been on holiday?"

"Yes, went to Majorca."

"Where's that?"

"I don't know, we went by air!"

Not only did my parents live in Aberayron but Uncle Godfrey Briggs, with his wife and two children lived in a lovely big country house called "Monachty" at Ciliau Aeron, a few miles away. I was fond of Uncle Godfrey. He and my Aunt used to take me to play tennis at other houses and at the Lampeter Lawn Tennis Club, at the right time of the year, of course. I also went to the occasional Hunt or County Ball.

The one effect that the voyage home in a meat ship had on me was to put me off lamb or mutton. The all pervading, greasy smell of frozen lamb seemed to get into everything, into ones clothes and into the cabin.

I have never been good at studying on my own. So the next thing was to see about going for a refresher course at a navigation school and getting extra tuition before sitting for the Board of Trade examination for 2nd mate. At a navigation school one learnt what to expect and how questions would be put. The tutors at the schools were well versed in the whims of the various examiners. If you got Captain So and So for Seamanship for example, he liked you to put the answers in a certain way. Even though we were to sit for an exam that would qualify us to be Officers in a steamship, many questions were put about handling a sailing ship, names of sails, and how to lower a broken topmast. Then there was the very important "Rule of the Road at Sea". There were 31 articles in the Rule of the Road and we had to learn them word perfect and by number. The candidate was always questioned very closely on the "Articles" as they were called. We had to repeat, word for word, the ones asked for and explain their applications with models on a table. Though I have never been able to memorise words easily, I remember some of these to this day. The Navigation papers were always written, but Seamanship was viva voce . It was very important, and I found this part the most difficult. Nearly everyone got cold feet about Seamanship. The penalties for failure in either subject were to postpone re-examination for up to six months.

I wanted to take the examinations in London. Liverpool, after two years on the Conway, did not attract me at all - besides I knew no one in Liverpool. Fortunately my Aunt Corrie came to the rescue. She was my father's only sister and had married, late in life, a Colonel in the Lancashire Fusiliers called Kelly Purnell, some twelve years younger than herself. They lived in a delightful detached house with a walled garden on the corner of Clifton Hill and Hamilton Terrace in St Johns Wood. My Uncle was a member of the M.C.C., and Lords was within walking distance down St Johns Wood Road. This began my education on life in London. My Uncle was also a member of the Naval and Military Club in Piccadilly. The "IN and OUT" as it was called, because its entrance from Piccadilly had two gates and a crescent shaped drive - the gates being named 'IN' and 'OUT'. Both Aunt and Uncle were fond of dancing and they also kept a very good house. There were two maids, a cook, and a house-parlourmaid. The latter was tall, good looking, and Irish. Her surname was Friel. It was usual to address staff by their surnames so I never knew her first name, even though I had two spells of living there; a couple of months each time.

It would be about this time that my social education began. Uncle and Aunt were sticklers for the right way of doing things, and as I am speaking of 1926, correct behaviour and dress were pretty formal. We usually dressed for dinner at night. You never went dancing, or to the theatre in day clothes if you were in good seats. I acquired an 'opera hat' to wear in the evening. This was a black top hat that folded down flat. Most theatre seats of those days were fitted with a wire rest underneath. Into this you slipped your folded down opera hat. An opera hat looked very smart at night, especially if the owner was wearing 'tails'.

I had served my time in Liverpool ships and had developed a slight Liverpool accent. Of the regional accents of Britain, Liverpool is one of the least pleasant to the ear. It is nasal, with Irish overtones and expressions. Today regional accents are accepted but in those days they were frowned upon, Scottish and Welsh excepted. However I pick up accents easily and lose them with equal ease.

I decided to go to a Navigation School in the East End of London, near the docks, the Sir John Cass School of Navigation and Seamanship. It was run by a man with an Extra Master's Certificate and situated in the Sailors Home in Commercial Road. It was quite a journey for me every day. It started with a bus along St Johns Wood Road to Baker Street Station, then the underground to Aldgate and then a bus or tram down Commercial Road. I was in no hurry, life was very pleasant. so I set myself six weeks to get ready for the exam. I attended school regularly during the day but did not do any work in the evening, except perhaps try to learn the awful "Articles" by heart.

I had other relatives in London. The one I knew best was one of my mother's sisters, Dr Ethel Vaughan-Sawyer. She was one of a very early generation of women doctors, a gynaecologist, and lived at 131 Harley Street. Two of her brothers married doctors. In her student days she must have introduced her brothers to her fellow students. I knew Aunt Ethel well. My mother and I had stayed with her many times, especially when we lived in Ireland. Her husband had been killed in the 1914-18 war and her only daughter died of food poisoning during a holiday in the South of France. Aunt was a well known and much respected specialist and stayed at 131 through the last war, even though the house was badly damaged during the blitz on London. She smoked Turkish cigarettes, almost continuously, and put away a good quota of whiskey. I remember once going to dinner with her and she would only allow me one whiskey because I had come by car and had to drive home. One of the few in those days who recognised the danger of mixing alcohol with driving a motor car.

I grew very fond of Aunt Corrie and Uncle Kelly and they were very good to me, even though I must have been a nuisance to them and an expense as well. They took me everywhere with them and treated me like a son. Army pensions weren't high in those days and my Uncle was always looking for a little extra to help out. He spent some time selling advertising space for the Christian Science Magazine and later they tried selling goods at a discount through Purnells Purchasing Co. They bought goods at trade prices for you, or sent the customer to Wholesale Houses who were willing to deal through them. I think they did quite well in this. However there never seemed to be a shortage of money and my Aunt had a reasonable income of her own.One day, during my first visit to them, my Aunt told me that a Mrs. Murray had telephoned to say she had heard my Aunt had a nephew staying and would he like to come to a small private dance as she was short of men. Mrs.Murray was the wife of a retired Colonel and they kept a private hotel in Leinster Gardens. They had a son who worked in a bank, and a daughter who was a doctor's secretary. I duly went to the dance which was quite small and held in one of the hotel's downstairs rooms. About 25 or 30 people were present and I was met by the daughter of the house. Oddly, I was immediately attracted. She was almost as tall as I was, with dark red hair, and brown eyes set in a fine strong oval face. Little did I know then that this was the girl with whom I was to celebrate our diamond wedding. There were to be a few ups and downs before then. Her name was Alice, though the family all called her Sis. There were two other Alices alive at the time - her mother and her grandmother. She had certainly grown out of being "little Alice" as she used to be called.I was busy at the navigation school all day and my new found girl, who was secretary to Andrew Wylie an E.N.T. specialist,worked in his rooms near the Langham Hotel in Queen Ann Street. We started going out together,occasionally, and our dancing styles seemed to fit naturally. Soon it was time to go for the dreaded examination which, fortunately, I passed easily some time before Xmas.

I was now certified as capable of carrying out the duties of 2nd Mate of a foreign going steamship. So it was home for Xmas and a letter to the Hall Line to say that I had got my "ticket" and please could I have a job. I did not have long to wait and in the new year, soon after my 20th birthday I was appointed 3rd mate of the steamship *City of Singapore,* which I was to join in Hull.

It was a difficult journey from Aberayron, buried in the West of Wales, to Hull on the East Coast. Nothing much went across England and I vaguely remember a very long and tiring journey, eventually arriving at the wharf at night, in pouring, rain and being greeted by the Chief Officer with one of the strongest Liverpool accents I have ever heard. The *City of Singapore* was a fairly standard size cargo ship of her day with a registered tonnage of 6567 tons, single screw triple expansion steam engines, fitted to burn either coal or oil fuel. Indistinguishable from my last ship, the *City of Winchester* had an Indian crew which was standard for all the Company's ships.

The ship had arrived from Rotterdam, having just had an almost complete rebuild. She had caught fire in Adelaide, a year or more earlier, and had been almost completely burnt out. The decision having been made that she could be salved, two Dutch tugs steamed out from Holland to tow her back to Europe. One of the longest tows of a disabled ship in history. She was almost immediately in trouble again after being repaired. She left the dock, the tugs cast off, and almost at once she ran into the bank of the river. It was then discovered that the oil pipes from the steering wheel on the bridge to the steering engine aft, which operated the engine, had been crossed. The result being that when the wheel was put one way the rudder went the opposite way. Imagine the consternation and despair this caused the pilot. However, it was soon put right, and no damage was done.

It was to be a happy ship and I became great friends with the second mate whose first name was Darcy. The one fly in the ointment was the first mate whose Liverpool accent was too much for us. We teased him, whenever this could be done without risking actual insubordination. One of our favourite methods was to "talk Liverpool" too. After some practice we became very proficient in this, with the subsequent disadvantage that, after a year, it was very difficult to lose the accent. I came home to my new found girl friend with this horrible accent.

From Hull we went to Middlesborough and one evening four of us were sitting in the bar of a pub somewhere near the ship when a large dog walked in and went up to our Chief Engineer. In his inimitable Scottish accent the Chief said "What a grand doog!!" One of us remarked that it was a dog not a 'doog'. This brought the reply which I have never forgotten. "If it's no a doog its verra like a doog." It was in this ship that we had a Scottish carpenter who we called "Nae Wid". Whenever he was asked to make anything his stock answer was "I've go' nae wid!!". The Scots were great seafarers and of course very many ships engineers came from the great shipyards of Scotland. There was a saying "If ye come frae Glesgae or bonnie Dundee you're sure of a job in the APOC" (Anglo Persian Oil Company, as it was then. It's now BP).

Officers accomodation on a large merchant ship of the day, was not luxurious but comfortable. The captain would have day and night cabins, usually just under the navigating bridge. If suddenly needed he would only have a few steps to go up a ladder to the bridge. The Chief Officer, Chief Engineer, and Chief Steward would have big cabins near the saloon. They needed space for their records and bookwork, and when in port space was needed for interviews with callers. Junior officers' cabins were comfortable and furnished with a bunk, fairly high, three levels of drawers underneath. At the end of the bunk there would be a wardrobe, thus taking up all one wall. Under the porthole, there was a desk, or table, and on the wall opposite the bunk there was a cushioned settee. At the end of the settee there was usually a folding wash basin in a cabinet. The top contained a water tank and under the basin a receptacle to receive the slops. Both were serviced by the steward. An electric fan, overhead and reading lights, steam heated radiator, completed the picture. If you took a little trouble this type of cabin could be made very homely.

Time has removed details of that voyage from my mind except that we commenced to load cargo for the U.K. in Japan. We went to Yokohama and then to Karatsu, a bitterly cold and barren spot in the Northern Island of Japan. We were anchored in the harbour loading from lighters. One morning a motor lighter with cargo workers came alongside, just as someone flushed a lavatory on board and the men in the lighter got the full benefit. They rushed up the gangway screaming at us and brandishing very savage looking cargo hooks. They demanded apologies from everyone and for some time the situation was quite unpleasant, especially as at that point they had no English and we had no Japanese. However, someone arrived who was responsible for the men and soon all was settled. It is a Japanese trait to demand abject apologies for wrongs or fancied wrongs done to them, and I was to meet this again later in my life.

The next part of the voyage I had never done before. We went from Japan to Vancouver where we loaded cases of tinned salmon, then on to Seattle and then miles up a great beautiful river to Portland, Oregon. There were tall trees on both sides of the river, timber mills, and neat white wooden houses along the river banks. We loaded timber in Portland and then went to San Francisco and San Pedro. At both places we loaded cases of tinned fruit and San Pedro saw us with a full cargo.

It was 1928, I had just had my 21st birthday and I saw that the RAF were advertising for Officers for short service commissions. I had long ago decided that at some point I would give up going to sea. These long, long voyages were not my idea at all of what life was meant to be about. I had acquired a girl friend, who I hoped one day I might marry, and had seen the sort of married life other sailors had to lead. The sea had less and less appeal. Though I loved going to sea, as such, and was deeply interested in ships and all about them. I had written to the Air Ministry and had got all the papers. I went to a doctor in Vancouver for a medical examination. All candidates were advised to do this before applying to save disappointment. Nothing however was to come of it because when I got home and told of my plans not only my father, but my girls' father came down on me like a ton of bricks. Everyone advised me to stick to what I had and not try to change. Anyway, it was 'only a short service commission and what then' and so on. It is never easy to fight ones family, so I eventually gave up the idea. Things began to change on the world scene, and those short service commissions became permanent for all those who wished to stay on in the RAF.

During the last war, when I was in the Royal Navy, I met an RAF Group Captain and found he had been in my term on *HMS Conway*, the training ship. I asked when he had joined the RAF and his reply was '1927', the time I would have joined. Looking back on it now I wonder whether I would have made a good pilot. I do not take stress very well, but I was extremely interested in the Services. They had always appealed to me. Certainly the Navy and the Air Force had. Though my attitude to the Army was rather like the old Navy Song "We don't want to march like the infantry etc... we are the King's Navee".

We left the West Coast of America fully loaded and sailed via the Panama Canal. Not long out of the Carribean area we ran into a gale, while still in the Southern part of the North Atlantic. Looking back now I realise that it was the worst gale of my seagoing experience. We 'hove to' with the ship being fully loaded. One stood on the bridge and watched these towering seas ahead. Seas that you had to look up to when you were already standing 25-30 feet above the level of the sea. The ship would rise most of the way to the top of a wave then crash, and a wall of water would collapse onto the forecastle and the ship would be under water as far as the bridge. The sun was shining and the beauty of the green-blue wall of the wave, with white on top was quite breathtaking but dangerous. These heavy seas worked the wedges holding the tarpaulin of No 2 hatch loose, and the tarpaulin began to come adrift. No one could go out on the foredeck and the only way to secure the hatch was to turn the ship round. Dangerous, but it had to be done. After we got the ship stern on to the wind the sea stopped breaking over the foredeck, the carpenter and the crew secured the hatch and hammered home the wedges keeping the tarpaulins in place. The danger of this manoeuvre is damage to the ship if a huge wave is taken on board while the ship is beam on to the sea. Once we had secured the hatch we turned the ship gently back to head the sea again on the original course. It was all over in 24 hours but unpleasant while it lasted. A big, well found, and fairly new ship is safe under most, even cyclone conditions, until something goes wrong. Many things that can go wrong, such as losing a hatch cover.

All Ellerman ships had Indian crews. Indian always, in the engineroom, though sometimes we had Chinese or Malays on deck. British ships were not supposed to take Indian crews into the North Atlantic in winter, or so I always understood, though we did. Most of us got a quick smattering of the language used by Indian seamen called "lascari bat" (sailors talk). The deck and engine room serangs, cassab (storekeeper), were petty officers and all spoke English, even if varying in intelligibility, but the sailors and stokers spoke very little and always addressed us in, (we called it), Hindustani. This was fairly simple but became complicated sometimes when we addressed them and it made no sense to them. I was working on deck one day and one of the Junior Engineers was overhauling a winch, nearby. Wanting some tool the Engineer went to the engineroom skylight and called "Nichi"? a voice from below answered "Ah, Sahib". The engineer Bring me up a burra (big) spanner. Ah, Sahib" again. After some time an Indian greaser arrived carrying a large hammer. The Engineer looked at it and then said, angrily, "I said a burra spanner, can't you speak your own bloody language"?. The poor bloke returned many steps down the engine room ladders and eventually returned with the appropriate spanner. The English picked up from us was, of course, often colourful. The Chief Officer and the Serang were discussing, one morning what work needed doing. Some small job cropped up which the Serang thought we (cadets) could do so he said to the Chief Officer. "Could the bloody boys do it?" Whereupon the Chief Officer blew up and explained that we must not be referred to like that! He had of course heard the Chief Officer use the expression many times.

The *City of Singapore* finally arrived in U.K. and I went on leave. Unfortunately I was just a few days short of the one years sea time I needed to be eligible to sit for the examination for 1st Mate. This was a bit of bad luck, and things were not all that rosy in the shipping world either. We were near the end of 1927. Anyway, I soon wrote and asked for another ship but was astounded to get a reply saying that they had nothing for me. Subsequently I heard that our last cargo of tinned fruit and salmon had turned out badly and a lot had been pilfered at the time of loading. Whether this was the cause of my getting the sack I never discovered. It was more likely the Chief Officer had begun to dislike me, as intensely as we disliked him, and put in a bad report.

This was about February, so I lived at home and bought a motor bike with money I had saved and with some family help. The red haired girl in London was now becoming part of my life and there were many early starts from Wales on the 240 mile journey to London. This would take me a good eight hours, it was difficult to average more than 30 m.p.h. on the narrow country roads of those days.

For reasons best known to himself, my father did not approve of my association with red headed ladies in far away London. Knowing this, and not wishing to have to put up with his disapproval - I did not tell him of the things I knew he would not like. I told my mother however,in whom I always confided my hopes, my fears, and all that I did. So when I said to her "I think I will go to London tomorrow", all she said was "I will get some lunch ready for you". My parents slept in different rooms and about 7.0 am my father, on hearing my motor bike start up, would rush into my mother's room saying "Where's the boy gone?" to which he got the reply "I think he has gone to London". However he always seemed pleased to see me when I got back, and peace reigned until I did something else of which he did not approve. I seem to have received a lot of disapproval, and very little encouragement.

After a while I had to have a job. I tried to get into the London Police but I was not allowed to marry for some years, so that was off. The Port of London Authority, where I had influence was no good either. Shipping companies did not want anyone. My father wrote to a cousin of his in Lancashire, who was a Rushton and manufactured machinery. He was shattered with the reply, which was to the effect that they did not have a job for me. Even if they did he would not employ a member of the family.

At last my letter writing and job applications paid off after someone suggested that I applied to the Naval Stores Department of Admiralty. After a satisfactory interview I had a job at last, at the end of July. I was appointed third officer of the Royal Fleet Auxiliary, *RFA Prestol.* Thus began a new period of my life and I left cargo carrying merchant ships behind for ever. Though not long voyages.

Chapter 4

NEW HORIZONS
1928 to 1932

My appointment to *RFA Prestol* in the Royal Fleet Auxilliary Service began a new period of my life. I left cargo carrying merchant ships for ever. However I was not yet free of long voyages and this was some time ahead.

A navy does not consist of warships alone. In the case of a large Navy such as Britain's, a number of auxiliary ships are required, storeships, oil tankers, ammunition ships and so on. Of these the most important and numerous are the oil tankers which were of two kinds; the overseas tankers that brought the fuel to Britain from various sources, and the fleet tankers whose job it was to supply oil directly to the fleet. This tanker fleet consisted of 1,000 ton ships for harbour duties, 2,000 ton ships also for harbour duties but able to move with the fleet, and 5,000 tonners which could be used to operate with the fleet and supply oil at sea, or carry oil from overseas to Naval storage at various bases the Royal Navy had around the world. In addition to these ships, specially built for the Navy, there was an assortment of commercial type ocean going tankers. A number of these were built during World War 1 and their names all began with "war" such as *WAR HINDOO*. There were a few other tankers acquired by the Admiralty at various times.

We were known as the Royal Fleet Axillaries, RFA's for short. The crews were all civilian and we were employed under the usual mercantile marine articles of employment. Everything we did was done the Naval way. The system of administration was exactly the same as that of an H.M. ship. We kept the same records as regards stores, repairs, accounting and all our repairs were done in Naval Dockyards and from whom we obtained our stores. We were in constant contact with the Navy, used Naval terminology and Naval signal flags. Much that I learnt during my time in the RFA's served me in good stead in later years.

I was to find, as time went on, that working for the Naval Stores Department was a very different thing to being in a commercial shipping company. The pace was much more relaxed. If you were in port, discharging into Naval oil tanks, over a week-end - well that was that - everyone knocked off and started again on Monday. Whereas in a commercial ship every effort had to be made to avoid being in port over week-ends and holidays. Once you had a job you could regard it as fairly permanent. Stores were easily obtained from the various depots and there was no difficulty in keeping the ships clean and smart. We were all painted the appropriate Naval grey of the station the ship was on. Dark grey for home fleet, and lighter greys for Mediterranean and China stations, except overseas tankers which were black and white. Last but not least, and something I regarded as important, it was only the overseas tankers that went deep sea. By this time I had become very attached to being ashore. Not only had I found a girl I intended to marry, but the novelty of long voyages had worn off. My idea of the good life was a ship that had a home port and only went to sea occasionally, or only went on short voyages. In fact I was a sailor who did not really want to go to sea.

On the 23 July 1928 I joined *RFA Prestol,* at Portsmouth, as 3rd Officer. It was good to have a job again and this was something new and it really captured my interest to be among the Navy that I had so much wanted to join as a boy.

PRESTOL was one of the 2,000 ton Naval oilers built in 1912, in Glasgow by Napier and Miller Ltd., 320ft long by 42ft beam. Engines and accommodation were amidships. We did not leave Portsmouth during the couple of months I served in her but most days of the week we went alongside one of the many H.M. ships in the harbour to top up their fuel tanks then, up to the oil depot to top up our cargo ready for the next demand.

Service in these base oilers was regarded by the Board of Trade as "Coastal", and the time spent on them did not fully qualify as sea time. This was recognised by the Naval Store Department and those officers who needed sea time were not kept for long in the base oilers. Looking back, I would say that they were good employers. Of course they never paid more than they had to and a 3rd Officer's pay was, including tanker bonus, £11-10 per month. Even in those days it was minimal. The R.F.A's are still sailing the seas and the Service has expanded considerably. I am glad to see that the old names of the fleet oilers have been perpetuated and I often see photographs of a much larger *ORANGELEAF* or *PEARLEAF* going about he business

After a couple of months a signal arrived to say that I was to be transferred to the *RFA Delphinula*, an overseas oiler that was then discharging a cargo from Trinidad at the oil depot in Portsmouth. Naturally I was pleased about this as I would soon be able to get my sea time in.

RFA Delphinula was an odd ship. I never discovered how or why the Admiralty acquired her. She started life as the Japanese *Buyo Maru*, was built before the Great War by Armstrong Whitworth and Co Ltd. of Newcastle. Her registered tonnage 4990. Engines were aft and officers' accommodation was amidships. She had a very unusual look with two rather thin funnels. She had four boilers and each pair of boilers had a separate funnel. Many cargo ships with two funnels are seen today but in 1928 it was very unusual. She was on a regular run carrying fuel oil for the Navy from Trinidad to various British ports where the Navy had an oil storage depot.

I did four months in *Delphinula* as 3rd Officer. Except for the first voyage it was a very happy ship. one remembers happy ships and various incidents stick in the memory, whereas unhappy ships seem to get forgotten. Happy memories were; off watch deck and engineer officers crowded into someone's cabin, singing songs, accompanied by the 4th Engineer playing his guitar, and our bridge sessions. We played Auction Bridge in those days. It was quite unusual for junior engineers to mix with the deck officers; but this ship was different.

Our Captain was new to the ship and there was no one on board who had sailed with him, so as far as we knew he was no different from any of the other captains we were destined to sail with. He was a fine man - large framed with a pleasant face and manner. He was very Scotch and came from the Shetlands, I think. A5 soon as we had cleared the English Channel he ordered his steward to bring him a case of gin - one dozen bottles - after which he was not seen on deck. Presumably this was quickly followed by another case and as his cabin was directly under the navigating bridge, the officer of the watch began to hear shouts and screams coming from the Captains cabin. As 3rd officer I kept the 8-12 watch am and pm. The ladder up to the starboard side of the bridge passed a square porthole into his cabin and if the shouts got loud I could go down the ladder a few steps and investigate. He would sometimes be sitting in his armchair watching something come down the wall and move towards him. As the thing got close he would leave his chair and start to crawl away, shouting or screaming at it. Sometimes I would see him just on his hands and knees. It was obvious that he either had D.T.'s or was on the way. During the day he mostly slept, but he was noisy at night during my watch.

Fortunately there were two ladders to the navigation bridge and I felt that if he came up one and wanted to attack me I could nip down the other.

About 9pm, I would hear stumbling footsteps on the ladder and the Captain would appear. Then my polite greeting "Good evening, Sir" A fuddled voice then asked "What are you steering?". "272, Sir", I would reply. Turning to the quartermaster at the wheel, he would order "Steer 275" The Quartermaster acknowledged the order but in fact, on my instructions, did nothing. Having done what I suppose he felt was his duty, he would stagger off down to his cabin for another drink. At no time did he ever seem to be aggressive. Though I did feel that I had to be extremely careful and not get into any cross purposes with him.

Being alone on the bridge, late at night, was not all that comfortable. The only means of communication were two voice pipes, one to the captain and one to the engine room. There was of course, the quartermaster at the wheel. It would not have mattered if he left the wheel while in mid-ocean. Somehow, it was the Chief Officer that I would have like to have been able to call.

About half way across the Atlantic the situation with the Captain got much worse and we were all very worried. The Chief Officer decided to order the Captain's steward to stop supplying drink. After 24 hours without a drink the Captain began to recover enough to demand gin. The steward finally had to admit that 'no more gin' was the Chief Officer's orders. The immediate result of this was "Tell the Chief Officer I want to see him". The Chief Officer duly arrived in the Captain's cabin. "We are getting towards Trinidad, Sir" he said "perhaps you should go easy on the gin". "You have no right to speak to me like that, its my business what I drink", was the reply. The argument was finally clinched when the Captain said "Who is in command of this ship? You or me?." The only reply could be "Well you are, Sir." The order then came "Tell my steward to bring me a case of gin".

It was a particularly difficult situation for the Chief Officer but he had our backing and support all the time. He had to take full responsibility for the situation whether he liked it or not.

Another few days, I think the voyage took about twelve days in all, in the most beautiful weather, well out of the gales of the North Atlantic. We were now approaching Trinidad. The entrance to the harbour at Trinidad was through a couple of rather narrow passages, between some islands. Called by Christopher Columbus, "Boca Tigris", into a large sheltered bay. The tides run strongly in and out and very careful navigation is required to negotiate the passage. It was forenoon and I was on the bridge with the Chief Officer. He had taken over the watch and was taking the ship into harbour. Who should suddenly arrive on the bridge but the Captain, the last person we wanted to see. He started giving orders which were properly acknowledged. In accordance with previous instructions no one took any notice of them. Fortunately, as before, the Captain went below when he felt that he had done what was necessary. The Chief Officer brought the ship to an anchorage to await the pilot, and the usual reception committee. This would include the ship's agent and the Customs Officers.

When the visitors arrived the Chief Officer had a long talk with the agent. The Captain had retired to his cabin. The agent went to see the Captain, and of course had a drink or two, and suggested the Captain come ashore for a run round the town. This seemed to be a great idea and the Captain agreed with alacrity. The agent's car and driver were waiting and off they went. After a while the car passed through large iron gates and up a drive towards a big red brick building. As the car stopped the Captain got suspicious, tried to jump out but was promptly grabbed by two huge black men in white coats. The agent had evidently been able to stop on the way and phone a warning, they were expected. It was the Trinidad Mental Hospital. That was the end of the Captain for that trip. The incident was reported by signal to Admiralty. The Chief Officer was instructed to assume command and bring the Ship home, loaded.

It was a quiet trip home and quite uneventful. For our next trip we had a new Captain - one whom we all liked. History does not relate what happened to the one we left ashore in Trinidad but it can be presumed the Admiralty had no further use for his services. It was an unforgettable and an unpleasant experience, and a sad one. He was a fine big man, pleasant and friendly when he was sober. It seemed sad to wreck a good career for a few bottles of gin.

We discharged that cargo at Milford Haven in to the Admiralty oil tanks there. I remember it was over a long weekend and Sis Murray, for that was her name (real name Alice), came down from London to see me. It was a long trip to make by train. This was the first time that she had visited one of my ships, and she was not at least impressed with the smell of an oil tanker. The all pervading smell of fuel oil, which we never noticed, she found hard to take. She arrived on a Saturday and took a room at an hotel. On Sunday evening I put her on a train back to London. In those days unchaperoned expeditions of that nature were rather frowned upon. However, she was not often deterred by what people thought of us and she was always prepared to fight her father if necessary. I am sure that she had to fight for her freedom that time, but she made light of it to me.

One more trip to Trinidad and except for some of the first trip, it had been a very happy four months. One could well ask "what effect did it have on your own relationship with alcohol?" I would reply "Well none really". It did, however, teach me the dangers of misuse and over the years I have seen much unhappiness caused by alcohol. For myself, I discovered, when I got into a hard drinking school on board a passenger ship, how dangerous it is and how difficult it is to pull yourself out of the mess.

At the end of four months in *Delphinula* I had acquired all the sea time I needed to enable me to sit for 1st mate. So, back to my uncle and aunt, and their very nice house in St John's Wood and also to the Navigation School for a few weeks to brush up on my work. I passed easily and I see that on 2nd. April 1929 I was appointed 3rd mate of the *RFA War Hindoo*. This was a really happy ship and I was to spend a total of 17 months in her. During that time Sis and I got married. It was a real blessing to have a home in London at which to stay during my time at the Navigation school. My Aunt and Uncle made no charge for my "board and lodging", which was a terrific help and it meant that I only had to pay for my school fees, travelling, and lunches. They treated me like a son and welcomed Sis Murray into their home as well. My Uncle was quite prepared to tick me off if he felt I needed it. By now I was very much involved with Sis and most evenings I wanted to spend with her. Eventually this became too much for my Uncle who gave me a good lecture on, "treating the place like a hotel". I am sure that I deserved it as at that age one is pretty thoughtless and up to a point I only thought of myself. One evening we were all sitting down to dinner when the phone rang. Friel, the parlourmaid, answered it and came back saying "Miss Murray on the phone again for Mr Christopher". My Uncle blew up at the "again" and poor Friel got a good ticking off. They gave me great care and much affection, taught me a lot about the social graces and took me everywhere with them and whenever we went dancing always included Sis. They owned an enormous bulldog named Rastus. He was a huge dog and a great pet. When my Aunt had a dinner party he had a habit or sitting under the table and snuffling and dribbling. Female guests in long dresses and others in black trousers did not always appreciate Rastus so my Aunt would provide little aprons to put over the knees. I used to take him for walks, and as long as we followed an established route he was quite happy and waddled along carefully inspecting each lamppost. However if I took him too far and he got out of an area with which he was familiar, he would sit down in the middle of the pavement and refuse to go on in either direction. This left an embarrassed young man anchored to a huge bulldog and receiving the amused comments of passers-by. Eventually I would be able to persuade him that we were not going any further and he condescended to waddle home.

It was about this time that my Aunt began to get worried. She had actively assisted in my association with Sis and up to the present all had gone well. Now she realized that things had got serious between us, and she was sure that it would not meet with my father's approval. In this she was quite right. She did her best to undo it, but by that time it was far too late. She was very fond of my father, who was her eldest brother, and knew that he had very fixed ideas about many things - particularly early marriage. His advice to me once had been, "never marry a red headed woman!" This was exactly what I proposed to do. At my age, too, the whole thing was most unlikely to win his approval. In addition to this, Sis's parents were not well off. Colonel Murray had retired from the Army just before 1914 and rejoined for the duration. He had a pre-war Captain's pension. He managed to educate his two children and after various enterprises settled down to work for an Insurance Company. To marry a girl who had no expectations of money was a great failure in my fathers eyes. So, all in all, the prospects of his blessing was pretty dim. My mother looked on things differently, and though she felt it was a pity about the money she was very pleased to have a prospective daughter-in-law. She had no daughter of her own which she was always sad about. She was also afraid that I would take up with a girl in the village. So it was under this, not very happy, family atmosphere that we decided to get married.

The *War Hindoo* was busy bringing oil from the Persian Gulf and it was to be my first experience of loading fuel oil at Abadan - which as far as I remember was the only oil port in the Gulf at that time. Even then there was a steady stream of tankers round Ras al Hadd and through the Strait of Hormuz. A dangerous area then as it is today. Haze from heat and dust caused poor visibility and lighthouses were few and far between. We were kept busy topping up the oil storage at Malta and Singapore for the Navy. The huge Singapore Naval Base had just been completed and the RFA's were kept busy filling the very large oil storage tanks there. Under very different circumstances. I saw these tanks in flames, not much more than ten years later.

There were several uneventful voyages to Malta and Singapore - mostly Malta. We never stayed any longer than the time it took to load or discharge, but there was usually time for some sight seeing and swimming in Malta. Abadan gave me my first taste of how hot some places were.

Loading in Abadan in the summer meant the ship got pretty red hot during the day and the oil came in nearly boiling. When loading at night the 2nd officer, or myself, took it in turns to be on duty which meant being about and alert as the tanks were being filled. The unforgivable sin was to let a tank overflow. It was nice and cool at night, or at least seemed cool, but when day came and you needed to sleep - a hot cabin made it difficult. I found it was possible to wrap oneself in a wet sheet and get to sleep. It may have been a dangerous thing to do but it was certainly effective. Much of my time was spent writing long letters to Sis. I wish some of them had survived the years - they would have been very useful to me now. None of the letters to my parents survived either. I wrote long letters to them as well. We were now planning to get married when the ship got home and of course there was much resistance from my father.

Sis' parents seemed quite happy about it all, or at least if they were not they put on a good face about it for Sis's sake. Colonel Murray wrote to my father. I understand it was a nice letter hoping all would be well etc. Father very ungraciously refused to accept the offered hand of friendship and replied saying that I was far too young and it was a bad thing financially, and socially. I think it was the latter that really riled the Colonel as it was quite unjust and even in England's narrow class divisions of that time - no one could say that Sis and I were not of the same class.

Sis wrote to the Rector of the Anglican church at Aberayron asking him to put up the banns. This does not seen to happen in Australia but in England the "banns" or the announcement of the marriage had to be read in the couples' respective churches for three Sundays before a licence to marry could be obtained. The rector asked my parents if this was all right. My father said no and the rector accepted this. However Sis was able to put it right in spite of my father and the banns were read - just in time. The banns were also read on behalf of Sis in Holy Trinity Church, Brompton, where we intended to get married.

Some time before we were married we had been to Holy Trinity. It was a huge church and at the time we went full. Prebendary Gough, a well known cleric of his day, was speaking about the evils of Communism and what was going on in Russia. At that time mass executions, tortures, and concentration camps were being discovered by the world - today they are accepted as part of life.

War Hindoo returned to Portsmouth before Christmas 1929 and was due for a refit. The Chief Officer went on leave first and I got my fortnight or whatever it was after he returned to the ship. Two weeks leave per year was all the seafarer was allowed in those days. Today the Australian seaman gets about six months leave a year to make up for all the work he does on Saturdays, Sundays and public holidays.

We were married at Holy Trinity, Brompton on 7 January 1930. Our guests hardly had any effect on the emptiness of the vast church. Sis and her father had to face the long walk up the wide aisle to where I was waiting with Sis' brother, Bill Murray, who was my best man. My father refused to attend and to his dying day had never met my in-laws. The reception was very kindly given for Sis by her great Aunt, Mrs Janie Osborne, in her house in Ennismore Gardens, quite close to the church. My mother, bless her, had come to London for the wedding even though her sight was by now very poor.

All went well, except that we went off without my wallet which I had given to Bill to pay for any contingencies. We sat on a seat in Hyde Park while the car went back for the wallet.

We decided to spend our honeymoon, of about a week, at Bournemouth. The next day we set off in a coach with our luggage and one of our presents - a portable HMV gramophone. It was fairly heavy, in a solid black case with metal bound corners and a carrying handle. I had put it up in a rack above one of the seats - not ours. During the journey we heard a crash and saw that the gramophone had come off the rack and fallen on the bald head of the man sitting underneath it. In spite of our abject apologies he was not at all pleased and had a nasty bump on his head.

Bournemouth in mid-winter is not much fun but we were happy getting to know each other and, I suppose making plans for the future. We both had jobs. Sis with her ear, nose and throat specialist in London and mine with the RFA's. At that period of world depression - if you had a job you stuck to it, gratefully, and shut up.

Soon it was back to the *War Hindoo* and the good news that I had been promoted to second officer. The new job was very interesting as the Second officer was responsible for all the navigational equipment. This included chronometers and charts. The chronometers had to be wound daily, there were three of them; the time checked by radio signals and their daily rate and total error entered in the chronometer book. Many hours were spent correcting charts from the latest "Notices to Mariners". I had now become the keeper of the middle watch. That is 12 to 4

S.S. City of Winchester. National Maritime Museum photo.

R.F.A. Prestol. National Maritime Museum photo.

both am and pm. I rather enjoyed it. You had the morning to do your work and it was usually quiet on the bridge in the afternoon. Everyone else was asleep. Similarly the midnight to 4 am was quiet with the Captain asleep and the whole ship quiet. I was now trusted to take responsibility and my opinion was often asked. I was in fact the navigating officer, but the other officers and the captain took sights too, so at noon we had a pretty good picture of where the ship actually was.

It was a short voyage this time - only just over six months. The world was stuck in the great depression of the 1930's and there was no money for anything. Pay for the merchant service had been reduced without any consultation with the seamen and officers. The Admiralty was as hard up as anyone and on the last voyage we had been steaming at eight knots, to save fuel, our most economical speed. This voyage the Admiralty had managed to get a charter for us and we were to go to Abadan and load fuel oil for wherever. One never knew the destination until arrival at the loading port. We had taken on a lot of extra charts of places we would not normally have gone to and this more work for me keeping them up to date.We did two charter voyages only. The first was to Bombay, and the next to Simonstown in South Africa.

We did one more voyage on Admiralty business. I think it was Singapore, and then headed for home and Portsmouth where we were due in early September. As we were approaching Portsmouth the Pilot boat came alongside with two women on board. Much to my joy one of them was Sis. The other was the Captain's wife. It was a beautiful September morning, I remember, and the two women were on the bridge with us as we steamed into Portsmouth harbour.

It appeared that Sis had arrived in Portsmouth the day before and spent the night at a hotel. In the next room was the Captain's wife, who of course knew various people in the dockyard, and was able to get the trip out in the pilot boat for them both. It was a joyous reunion and Sis spent the night on board but did not enjoy the smell of the fuel oil as we were now alongside the oil berth. She never got used to the smell of oil tankers, whereas we never noticed it after a while. Even today the smell of heavy fuel oil brings brings back nostalgic memories to me.

I now had to get my Master's certificate. It was very much an unwritten rule that you didn't get married until you had passed for master. I broke the rule and did not pass for master first time. We had taken a large bed sitting room at Swiss Cottage and Sis went on working while I studied. By this time we had acquired a car. Spencer the Chief officer had bought a small second hand 9 H.P. Swift with the number TP251 to use while on leave. At the end of his leave he sold it to me for £11-10 ($23 Australian today) but nearly a months wages then for me. We went to Portsmouth to collect it, and at the same time said goodbye to Captain Williams, Chief Officer Spencer, and a very happy ship.

In a very old notebook I found the following account:-

Cost of car	£11.00.0
Half cost new tyre	17.6
New battery	1.15.0
Total	13.12.6
Paid to Mitchell	1.10.0
Garage near U.gate	4.0
New hub caps & fitting	17.6
Total	2.11.6

Car cost	13.12.6
To pay Spencer	£11.01.0

I had a driving licence but had not driven a car any distance before. However, I got on all right, my years of motor cycles made the traffic part of it easy, but handling a car and gear changing without synchromesh took a bit of getting used to. This was to be our first real experience of living together for any length of time. Our bed sitter was a big front room on the ground floor of a large house in a quiet street at Swiss Cottage. There was a "mews" nearby where we were able to keep the car. The London "mews " had been turned into garages, or in some cases into very pretty little houses. The room was quite big enough, nicely furnished with a double bed, large table in the middle, easy chairs, gas fire and behind a screen the sink and gas cooker.

We settled down to a routine of Sis to work, and me to my Navigation school in the East End of London. I was supposed to study in the evening but this did not get the application and continuity it deserved. We did a lot of dancing. I remember one evening we were to go out and decided to have a good hot bath. The bathroom had a penny in the slot gas water heater called a geyser. Each time the water began to cool off we put in another penny until we were both quite boiled and too sleepy to go out. The end result was that when I sat for the examination I passed in navigation but failed in seamanship. This I would have to do again in three months time. The seamanship examination was oral and I found oral exams difficult. It is so easy to be nervous and answer too quickly without sufficient thought and the seamanship required for master was very extensive and included a lot of what is called master's business. Most important if one is to take command of a merchant ship visiting foreign ports.

We were now presented with a problem. What were we to do for three months until I could sit again for my ticket?. We had the little car and Sis had her job, but we were paying rent and what we really needed was some cheap living. I suppose I could have gone back to sea, but never considered that. Going to sea was something you did as little as possible. It was a big decision to make but Sis decided to give up the job she had had for 8 1/2 years. We then packed up our first home together and went off to Wales to stay with my parents. They had been pressing us to stay and this had been impossible up to the present with Sis' job in London. I don't know what we did for cash. We must have had a few pounds of savings between us because we were able to run the car and meet our immediate needs. We had a pleasant couple of months in Wales. It was Christmas time and there was plenty to do. We even went to a hunt ball.

It was such a cold night that the car, in spite of being covered in rugs, refused to start. Some boiling water for the radiator, a good push from our amused fellow guests and off we went. The ball was held at the magnificent old home of Sir Lewes Pryse, an uncle of my Uncle Godfrey's second wife. This old and very beautiful house was called Goggerdan. Together with the estate, it is now the agricultural school of Aberystwyth University.

Returning to London we stayed with Sis's parents who now lived at Kenton, an outer suburb, near Harrow in Middlesex. This certainly continued our cheap living but was not in the best interests of family relationships. My father-in-law was a kind man who had struggled hard since the Great War to educate his small family, of whom he was very proud, and to care for them as best he could. He had, however, a temper not often roused but when it was - it was look out. One evening he and I were in the sitting room together and he had bent down to poke the coal fire. I lit a cigarette and flipped the match into the fire just past his nose. That was it. He blew up

CERTIFICATE OF COMPETENCY

MASTER

OF A FOREIGN-GOING STEAMSHIP

AS

To *Christopher Briggs*

No 307103

WHEREAS it has been reported to us that you have been found duly qualified to fulfil the duties of Master of a Foreign-going Steamship in the Merchant Service, we do hereby, in pursuance of the Merchant Shipping Acts, grant you this Certificate of Competency.

BY ORDER OF THE BOARD OF TRADE, this 4th day of *February* 19 31.

One of the
Assistant Secretaries
to the
Board of Trade

Countersigned

Registrar General

REGISTERED AT THE OFFICE OF THE REGISTRAR GENERAL OF SHIPPING AND SEAMEN.

(7299)

and called me all the things he could think of. Sis heard the row and valiantly came in on my side. She had always been prepared to stand up to him and this time she had her husband to defend as well. Finally she said that we would leave next day. Her father must have considered that this would be a great loss of face for him and finally there were apologies all round. In all my life no one before or since has ever been so angry with me. Throwing the spent match was a thoughtless gesture but these actions are almost automatic and I never foresaw the consequences.

On the 26 January 1931 I passed for my Masters Certificate. I was so elated that on my way home from the examination I stepped off the pavement in front of a taxi and it was only the skill of the taxi driver and the grace of God that I remained alive to benefit from it.

One more trip to sea, this time as 2nd officer in the *R.F.A. War Brahmin* to collect a load of fuel from Abadan. I had only to wait a few days, after I had informed the Naval Stores Department that I had passed my exam, before they had a ship for me. I have been lucky I suppose. The only time I have been out of a job in my life was when the Ellerman Hall line would not re-employ me after the *City of Singapore*. Perhaps that was lucky in many ways. My move out of merchant ships proper gave me a new perspective and I moved to an area that was different from normal sea going. We were in constant contact with the Navy and provided that your face and behaviour fitted, many officers were prepared to be friendly and welcome you on board their ships.

When we reached home, the *War Brahmin* was ordered to discharge at Plymouth. The oil tanks and the oiling jetty was at Tor Point on the Cornish side of the estuary. Sis came down to the ship on our arrival and as we were married she was allowed to stay on board while we discharged.

That was to be my last voyage in *War Brahmin* and I was sent on leave and appointed to the *RFA Scotol* on completion of my leave. Scotol was one of the one thousand ton class of base oilers. Small tankers with engines aft and bridge and accommodation forward. We were attached permanently to Portland and could live ashore and only pay for such meals as we had on board. Portland was the home of the anti-submarine establishment and the harbour was the home of a flotilla of submarines and another of destroyers. We were by no means overworked and usually the destroyers came alongside us when they needed to top up after exercises.

We were able to set up a home again. We found a bed sitting room first, just outside Weymouth, and after a few weeks found a bungalow at Wyke Regis. We had our little old 9 H.P. Swift car, Sis's little black spaniel, and our wedding presents to use, really for the first time. It was quite an idyllic time - we started off in September and were there until January. We were able to have members of the family to stay, and at Christmas Sis's parents came to spend Xmas with us and also my brother -in-law Bill Murray.

Time passed swiftly and I made friends with some of the destroyer officers. They invited me out on anti-submarine exercises which was quite exciting. This reinforced my deep regret that I had not been able to join the navy at the right time.

As 2nd officer on the *Scotol* on what was called "weekly rate" I seemed to be quite well off with some £16 a month. We now decided on a better car. We have somehow always been able to persuade ourselves that we needed a better car or even a new car. We got £5 trade in on the Swift and bought for £25 a four seater Riley tourer. This was a very good car, or at least it was until the Chief Engineer of my ship suggested I use his engine oil in the motor. A bit stupid of both of us because the lubricating oil used for a steam engine is a very different oil from that required for a petrol motor. The result was that the engine deteriorated fairly rapidly.

All good things come to an end and we had to pack up the bungalow at Wyke as the ship was to go round to Portsmouth for the annual refit. At the same time I was informed that I was to go on leave from Portsmouth and then take passage to Hong Kong and join the *RFA Belgol* as 3rd officer. Not only was this demotion but it meant that I would be away from home for three years. What is more, on the pay I would be getting, (eleven pounds ten shillings a month), there was no possibility of being able to pay my wife's passage to Hong Kong or live ashore if she got there.

We were devastated. That is the only way I can put it. Married life had fallen into place and our regard for each other was growing stronger as time went by. The thought of a three year separation was an awesome prospect. The alternative was unemployment. The world in 1932 was in the middle of the great depression. There were hunger marches in Britain, starving people in America, and laid up ships choked quiet anchorages. If I should reject the posting to Hong Kong there was no alternative except a soul destroying search for work. Now we were married we had gone beyond expecting much help from our families - neither of which was well off anyway.

We made two decisions, one was to accept the job in Hong Kong and hope a better job might turn up, and secondly to start a family. So, after the saddest of good byes - I sailed in the P. and O. *SS Mooltan* for Hong Kong. Never before or since have I ever been so desolate at parting. The prospect of life in Hong Kong, on eleven pounds ten a month, nine pounds of which I sent home, was pretty grim.

I had been to Hong Kong before, and to the places we stopped at on the way out so there was not much that was new. The work of *Belgol* was not exactly exciting. Hong Kong was the base of the China Squadron and consisted of an aircraft carrier, the *Hermes,* sunk by the Japanese in the Bay of Bengal in 1942, cruisers, destroyers, a submarine flotilla with their depot ship *HMS MEDWAY* and last but not least *RFA Belgol* the base oiler. Our routine was the same as that of the other base oilers. Destroyers would come alongside us for fuel and we would go alongside the bigger ships.

The squadron had a summer base at Wei Hai Wei in Shantung province on the North coast of China. There is a large bay at Wei Hai Wei and across the entrance to the bay an island. It was this island that had been leased to Britain. The Chinese city was on the mainland and the wide sweep of the bay gave a safe deep water anchorage. The Union Jack flew on the island and there were a few houses. Some, such as the Admirals house, and one or two others were official. There were some smaller houses available for rent. A hotel, clubs of course for officers and men and, some playing fields and storehouses.

In the summer Wei Hai Wei had an idyllic climate. When Hong Kong was wet, hot and steamy and you could barely sleep at night the change for the ship's crews to the cool Northern summer must have seemed heaven sent. I had joined *Belgol* in March and about May we loaded up and went to join the fleet at Wei Hai Wei. We stayed for a couple of weeks and when our tanks were empty returned to Hong Kong. I spent most of my time on board as my two pounds ten a month barely covered my bill on board ship, and there was nothing left over for entertainment.

Sis had a cousin in the Chinese Maritime Customs who was stationed in Shanghai and was fairly senior. He had been told that I was in Hong Kong but I had never met him. One day towards the end of June I got a letter from him, his name was Douglas Murray. The letter asked if I would like a job with the Customs, they were recruiting men with Master's Certificates for a fleet of preventive patrol ships now being developed. This may have been an answer to a prayer - it was certainly the concerted wish of the two of us to get together. My reply was immediate and I was told to report to the Commissioner of Kowloon Customs for an interview. This I did and at the end of the interview was told that I was acceptable. "How soon can you join us? One

R.F.A. Delphinula. National Maritime Museum photo.

R.F.A. War Hindoo. National Maritime Museum photo.

of our ships is here now and could take you to Shanghai." I went back to my ship and the Captain who was rather a friend, seemed very pleased and congratulated me on my good luck. The next move was to ask the SNSO (Senior Naval Store Officer) who was our boss, to signal Admiralty for my release. It all seemed too easy until the reply came to the effect "Briggs may be released on refund of £72 being pay and passage from U.K. to Hong Kong." Now the worry began. £72 was an astronomical sum in my circumstances. Sis applied to my father, who flatly refused and commented that he did not approve of me changing jobs anyway. Though she made a number of phone calls to him, he was adamant about it.While this was going on I sat on board the ship biting my nails and wondering if the great opportunity I was offered was going to be missed for want of seventy two lousy quid. The future that I saw was, a reasonable salary at last, the chance to bring my wife and child out to China and make a home together, and finally the chance to give up going on long voyages forever. The prospect was being able to live in some China coast port, go to sea for a few days and home again for a few days. All this hung in the balance.

All was not lost because just in time a signal came from *SMSO* to say "Briggs to be released forthwith". No one was happier than I. It turned out that Mrs.Murray, my wife's mother had put up the money and I was to pay it back at £6 a month. I reported to the Commissioner of Chinese Customs in Hong Kong and was told to take myself and my baggage on board *CPS Chunhsing* which was to sail for Shanghai the next day. My farewells to *Belgol* were quickly said, and with my heart filled with the pleasure of my good fortune, I stepped out of the sphere of the Royal Fleet Auxiliary Service into that of the Chinese Maritime Customs. The *Belgol's* motor boat took me and my baggage over to the *Chunhsing* in fine style. However I was not to be away from Hong Kong for long.

Chapter 5

HAI KUAN - The Sea Gate
1932

The *Chunhsing* was a new ship, built in Shanghai in 1927, and designed as a lighthouse tender. There were comfortable cabins for the officers, a large wardroom, and aft there were more comfortable cabins for passengers and a suite for V.I.P's. The passengers may consist of lighthouse keepers and their families, lighthouse engineers on inspections and maintenance tours, and occasionally a senior man from the Marine Department on an inspection trip. Space was provided for carrying cargo to the light stations and for plenty of boats. Big motor boats for towing and cutters for landing stores. I was a supernumery for the trip to Shanghai and I had one of the passenger cabins. The few days of the trip were spent learning about the Customs and how the ships were run.

The Chinese Maritime Customs was a unique service - its staff of dedicated Chinese and foreigners worked together in complete harmony and in a great spirit of loyalty and integrity. Everyone was well paid according to their position and the salary standards of the day.

From the Chinese Customs modest beginning in 1854 it developed over the years into China's foremost revenue collecting agency and a guarantee for the servicing of the Government's foreign and domestic financial obligations. Due to the Customs Service the Chinese Government were able to erect lighthouses and aids to navigation along the country's coasts and waterways, and up to the time of the Japanese war of 1941 the China coast was one of the best marked in the world with numerous modern lighthouse and wireless beacons. The sunken rocks and shifting shoals of the great Yangtze were marked by lightships, buoys, and beacons all regularly tended by the Marine Department's river launches.

The cosmopolitan staff, its wide range of interests, its ideals of service were quite unique and it continually worked for the advancement of the Chinese people.

To begin the long and interesting history of the Chinese Maritime Customs we need to go back to 1840 when the bargain system of paying duties, the unjust exaction of moneys, the inequality of treatment, the greed of underlings, and the squalor and corruption at the Custom House created grievances which ended in a war.

The Treaty of Nanking in 1842 put an end to the old system and opened five ports to foreign trade, each with its own Custom House. It provided for a fixed tariff on imports and exports and merchants could trade freely, providing they paid their dues.

The Customs Houses were not run on Western civil service lines and there was constant friction. It mattered little how many treaties were signed, the Chinese, even if willing, were unable to fulfil their treaty obligations. The many foreign traders were only there for their own good and were quick to take advantage of any breakdown in the customs system. Great reform in the whole customs area was urgently needed.

In March 1853 the Taiping rebels defeated the Imperial army and declared Nanking to be their capital. Shortly afterwards the native city at Shanghai was seized and a mob of bandits swarmed into the British Settlement, now quite large, and looted the Custom House thereby putting an end to it operation. The Shanghai Taotai (head man) fled and his staff dispersed.

The various merchants thought this was fine and that they were about to enter an era of free trade and no customs. However they were soon to be disillusioned. The Consuls of Britain and America came to the rescue and set themselves up as temporary Custom Houses, and foreign traders were ordered to pay the requisite duty at the various Consulates. This system soon broke down and there was much discussion as to what should be done. Eventually on the 25th of June the Taotai and the British, French, and American Consuls held a meeting to draw up regulations for the reorganisation of the Custom House. That meeting was the beginning of the modern Chinese Customs Service.

The original charter by which the Chinese Government accepted foreign aid in the administration of the Customs was the minutes of that meeting and the understanding that the new arrangements were a reorganisation and not a supersession of the Chinese Custom House. However the responsibility and authority were to remain in Chinese hands and the foreign Commissioner was to have a Chinese colleague, the Superintendent of Customs, and it remained this way until the revolution in 1911. The Superintendent actually received, banked and took charge of the money paid in as revenue.

The Chinese Government accepted the appointment of a Board of Inspectors who therefore became Chinese officials. One each from the French and American consulates and the British Vice-Consul Thomas F.Wade, all took the oath of office on 12th July 1854 and the Chinese Maritime Customs was born. Wade (later Sir Thomas) resigned in 1855 and was succeeded by a very forceful character Mr.Horatio Nelson Lay. He was a Vice-Consul and interpreter at the British Consulate in Shanghai. Honest and efficient administration was now in place, honest merchants were protected and the Chinese Government received valuable revenue.

This excellent arrangement had its drawback because the efficient revenue collection disadvantaged Shanghai, and merchants started using other Treaty Ports where the same old easy methods prevailed.

There had been further hostilities in China in 1856 and this led to the signing of the Treaties of Tientsin in 1858 by Britain, France, America and Russia. Resulting in the opening of ten more ports, it stipulated that the customs system adopted at Shanghai should be extended to all ports open to foreign trade. At this time, Horatio Lay, who had the task of putting all this into effect, changed his official title of Chief Commissioner into that of Inspector General and the American and French Commissioners of early days were paid off.

Canton was the first port to be reorganised and in October 1859 Lay opened the new Custom House and the first Commissioner was G.B.Glover, an American. The Deputy Commissioner was Mr.Robert Hart who had resigned from the British Consular Service to take up the appointment. This was the beginning of Hart's 50 years in the Chinese Customs Service described as "a career without parallel in the annals of the Far East, during which he was able to do more for the land of his adoption than any other foreigner before or since and, in doing so, to play no small part in the world's history."

The treaties required the payment of indemnities from Customs revenue to both Britain and France and accurate accounting was needed in this. Centralised arrangements were needed and it was considered that the chosen foreigner for this task should be the Inspector General of Customs and he should be appointed by the Tsung Li Yamen or Bureau of Foreign Affairs. Lay got the job and was appointed by Prince Kung, the head of the Yamen, in January 1861. However Lay had been ill and was sent on leave and did not return to China until 1863. In the meantime

Hart had been appointed Officiating Inspector General.

Lay had been authorised to purchase seven foreign style gunboats while in Britain but after his return to China he got himself into trouble with the Government over the control of the fleet and was dismissed. However generous financial treatment softened the blow.

Robert Hart was appointed Inspector General in November 1863 and this was received with acclaim by all sides of the community as by his ability and tact he was held in high regard by everyone. Prince Kung summoned him to Peking and he was told to take up residence there. It is said that " the problems facing the Peking Government, engendered mainly by the operation of the treaties and persistent foreign pressure, were growing so complex and urgent that it had become essential to have close at hand a counsellor well versed in foreign ways and on whose advice complete reliance could be placed."

After drawing up the General Pilotage Regulations in 1868 Hart had the idea that he should build up a vigorous Marine Department. He was a cautious man and never took a step unless he knew exactly where he was going but by 1911 he had succeeded in this and his Marine Department had a personnel of 895 of whom 114 were foreigners. The Department had 132 lighthouses, 45 light vessels and light boats, 138 buoys, 119 beacons and a flotilla of light tending and surveying steam vessels; quite an achievement in a little over 40 years. In 1882 he became Sir Robert Hart when he was created KCMG.

In 1886 the Hong Kong Government permitted the opening of an office of the Chinese Customs in the city of Victoria where a Commissioner of Customs of British nationality could function as the Chinese official in charge of the Kowloon district, and all Chinese revenue collecting agencies within its limits. At this time the Portuguese enclave of Macau was still not, after 330 years, Portuguese territory. However in March 1887 the Protocol of Lisbon was signed by which China confirmed the occupation of Macau and its dependencies by Portugal. This enabled the Chinese Customs to open a Custom House at Lappa to cover the Macau area in April 1887. By this time the Chinese Customs Service had grown to a little over 3000 Chinese and 685 foreigners.

China had during the 19th century continuous trouble with her dependencies and her tributary states such as Liuchiu, Formosa, Nepal, Burma and Annam. Then the political situation in Korea became dangerous and ended in all out war between China and Japan. This ended with the Treaty of Shimonoseki in April 1895 and China had to recognise the complete independence of Korea and pay a heavy indemnity which was to be a charge on the Chinese Customs revenue. Next year another treaty saw the cession of Formosa to Japan and the opening of four more Treaty Ports.

The use of steam vessels to ply and to trade in inland waters of China had been a contentious issue for some years and after the Treaty of Shimonoseki, which stipulated Soochow and Hangchow as Treaty Ports (both on inland waters), the situation became critical and new regulations were called for. In March 1898 Hart drew up comprehensive regulations for steam navigation inland and I quote "the year in which the Powers by individual and syndicated bullying, forced concession after concession from the Chinese Government". Among these proposed concessions was that of permitting foreign-flag vessels to trade to inland places which was demanded by the British Minister as part compensation for China's refusal to accept Great Britain's offer of a guaranteed loan. Whatever was done the Powers demanded more and eventually in 1901-02 the regulations were amended to allow sea going vessels to navigate inland waters which had been forbidden under the 1898 regulations.

The cession of Kowloon established by the Convention for the Extension of Hong Kong was signed in June 1898 and by October 1899 the customs stations in Kowloon were finally closed and China had to establish new Customs Stations on the Sumchun River and East and West of Hong Kong as I have described elsewhere.

The Sino-Japanese war of 1894-95 was the beginning of a period of great pressure on the Chinese Government by the foreign powers. Demands to be allowed to build railways, demands for the opening of interior waterways and then carving off large slices of Chinese territory, even though only on lease. All this aroused resentment and anti-foreign feeling. The British and Americans sent troops and ships to guard their Legations and their interests. There were anti-missionary demonstrations as well as riots and armed uprisings.

The sections of the populace who had reason to distrust and dislike the foreigners formed themselves into a society called I Ho Chuan or Boxers. The Boxer rising has been well documented. It all ended with China being forced to pay a huge indemnity secured on the Customs which forced an increase of the tariff up to 5% *ad valorem*.

The revolution came in 1911 and the Customs Service went through many changes and uncertainties but was continually sustained by the wisdom of Sir Robert Hart and his loyal acceptance of change. He died in 1911 and I quote in full what Foster-Hall had to say about this great man. "He had given his life to China, and with unswerving singlemindedness of purpose had devoted all his great gifts to her service. He had watched the country of his adoption emerge from her ancient state of seclusion into a modern age of untrammelled intercourse with all the nations of the earth, and at every stage of this painful progress he had always been ready to render the aid of sound guidance. He was a staunch upholder of the desirability of a united China, and as the trusted head of the Customs Service he had the satisfaction of seeing that Service, as its activities spread throughout the Empire, recognised not only as the sign and symbol of the Central Government's authority but also as, in a very real sense, a unifying agency. Holding the position he did, and having constant intercourse, both social an official, with men of every nationality, a man of Hart's ability could hardly fail to be a thorough cosmopolitan. An international outlook was indeed essential if the Service was to be run without needless friction and misunderstanding, and Hart saw to it that men selected for responsible posts either had or acquired this outlook. Long before internationalism had become a recognised ideal in world politics, Hart had already built up, with men from almost every nation in the world, the first great international service, and had inspired the men of this Service with the ideal of loyalty to China and the furtherance of China's interests. Unsought - for Hart was dowered with sublime humility which is so often the crown of genius - honours came to him in profusion. China showered distinctions on him, including such rare honours as the Red Button of the First Class, the First Class of the Second Division of the Order of the Double Dragon, Ancestral Rank of the First Class for Three Generations, the Peacock's Feather, and , most coveted of all, the title of Senior Guardian of the Heir Apparent. His own country gave him the GCMG and a baronetcy while of his numerous other honours conferred by other countries no fewer than 11 were grand crosses."

Hart was succeeded by Sir Francis Aglen and he was to carry the Customs through a very difficult period after the revolution which destroyed the Ching Dynasty and the subsequent years of disorder and partition by war lords when the 'government' in Peking had little or no control. Aglen left the Service in 1926 and the next three years saw control by A.H.F .Edwardes as Officiating Inspector General. Frederick W.Maze (later Sir Frederick) who was a nephew of Sir

Robert Hart became Inspector General in 1929 and the service saw more changes. One important one was to employ more Chinese and fewer foreigners and the new National Government under Chiang Kai Shek was granted tariff autonomy.

China quickly imposed much higher tariffs in place of the old 5% rates with the result that a fleet of fast preventive ships was required to deal with the smuggling and this is where I came in, in 1932, to be part of this force.

After the Japanese invasion in 1937 the Chinese Government moved to Chungking and wanted Maze to withdraw all Customs staff to new stations inland. Maze did not agree and pointed out that this would merely make it easier for the Japanese to take economic control. In the end the British Commissioner in Shanghai was not replaced until November 1941 and of the sixteen Customs establishments in the occupied area only four had Japanese Commissioners.

The head of the Marine Department enjoyed the title of Coast Inspector. Under him were two Deputy Coast Inspectors, an Armaments officer and an officer in charge of the Chart Department. The staffing of the department was predominantly British, Scandinavian and Danish. The Marine Department was on the 4th floor of the Customs House on the Bund in Shanghai. The Coast-Inspector had a delightful office in the corner with windows looking down on the busy Whangpoo River. The multitude of traffic big ships, little ships, junks, sampans was a never ending sight that one could stand and watch for hours, the river was a dark chocolate colour and the tides ran strongly. The Whangpoo is a tributary of the great Yangtze river and joined it at Woosung some 30-40 miles from the sea.

The Marine Department was responsible for the building and maintenance of all the lighthouses on the China Coast, the pilotage on the rivers, and some of the harbours, and the maintenance of all navigational aids, including buoyage. At Shanghai there was a spacious and well equipped buoy yard across the river at Pootung and almost opposite the Customs House. This area is now called Poodong New Area and is a 200 square mile complex of industrial parks, foreign factories and housing developments. The Yangpu bridge now connects Poodong with Shanghai. Upstream there is another bridge and a vehicle tunnel under the Whangpoo river. Within the Marine Department was an up to date Chart and Survey office, whose responsibility was to keep China Coast Charts up to date and the Customs ships carried out many minor surveys along the coast.

With the opening to foreign trade of the inland waterways the Customs was faced with the massive task of erecting and maintaining navigational aids for the Yangtze River from the sea to the head of navigation. It should be observed that the Yangtze is navigable for ocean going vessels as far as Hankow (now Wuhan) some 800 miles from the sea and for specially constructed river steamers for another 4-500 miles. A constantly changing river with the famous gorges and rapids in the upper reaches and there are floods and quickly changing sand banks in the lower reaches. To maintain navigational safety on the river was a never ending task and kept a large staff and many launches fully occupied the year round.

The concern of the Marine Department, to which I belonged was not originally with smuggling. Up to the present this had been fairly minor and except for launches attached to some of the ports the work of the Customs ships had all been the maintenance of light stations. The scene was now to change and the Marine Department were instructed to build up a sea going preventive force of small armed patrol vessels.

For once I was in the right place at the right time and how glad I was that I had not refused to go to China when the Admiralty had appointed me to the *RFA Belgol* in Hong Kong. A rapidly expanding fleet meant scope for quick promotion and as I had my master's ticket, I looked forward to the chance of a command of my own at an early age. Looking back on it now it was certainly the best job that I ever had. It was to be a job that I enjoyed, interested me and one with which I was compatible. The system was that the ships were based on a particular port and went to sea for so many days, then returned for a few days in port. This solved for me the contradiction of a stable home life with my family and my love of ships and the sea. The sea gets into the blood and once hooked the sailor hankers for it and yet also wants to be at home.

I duly arrived in Shanghai and reported for duty and an interview with the Coast Inspector. All went well and I met for the first time Louis Carrel, who was Coast Inspector, for whose encouragement and faith in my capabilities I am forever grateful. As years went by we were to become personal friends of Louis and Lucy Carrel and spent many pleasant evenings in their home in Shanghai.

The Secretary of the Coast Inspectorate was a man named Gander who had married a very charming Eurasian lady. Officially there was no such thing as racism in the Chinese Customs and we Europeans had Chinese over us, under us, and equal to us in rank. It was different though with the mixed race community who, unfortunately, were not accepted by either. I was to learn this in no uncertain terms when some months later a friend of mine, who was also a friend of the Ganders, took me, as a new boy, along to dinner on a Sunday with them and to the Cinema. A popular entertainment in Shanghai, Sunday night dinner and the pictures. It so happened that Lady Maze, the wife of the Inspector General of Customs, Sir Frederick Maze also had a dinner and picture party and were sitting not far behind. My wife's cousin Douglas Murray was in her party. Lady Maze turned to Douglas and inquired "who is that with the Ganders?" Douglas replied "Oh, that is Christopher Briggs who has just joined the Marine Department, his wife is a first cousin of mine." Today it is hard to believe but Lady Maze turned to Douglas and said "tell him that his wife may not be accepted here, when she comes out, unless he changes his friends." As the years went by it happened that we had a number of mixed race, or Eurasians as they were called, friends but mainly in Hong Kong and not in Shanghai.

It seemed that I was to remain in the *Chunhsing* as third officer for the time being and for training. A number of new ships were being built but none were quite ready. Our next trip was to be to the North tending the lighthouses on the way and calling in at Wei Hai Wei and Chefoo. My first taste of lighthouse tending. It was fairly primitive in those days. The stores were loaded into the ships boats and towed in to the landing place, sometimes sheltered but often very open to the weather. The unloading of stores and fuel usually took a couple of days and meanwhile the lighthouse engineers we had on board tested and inspected all the machinery. There was quite a lot of machinery,starting with the clockwork for the revolving lenses. It is this revolving beam of light which allows the lighthouse to give it's timed flashes. The lantern itself which would be a powerful kerosene pressure lamp. Then there was often a generator and pumps and finally the big diesel engine that ran the air compressor for the foghorn. It was all new to me and I found it particularly interesting. Each lighthouse was different and we exchanged keepers and their families as well as landing supplies.Chefoo, with its neat little harbour nestling under the Bluff, was the end of our journey. We were to stay there some days. Everything we did was at a delightfully leisurely pace, not the in and out of port rush as was usual in merchant ships.It was summer time and the American Navy was at Chefoo in force. This meant the town was alive. Cabaret girls from the Shanghai dance halls arrived in force for their summer holidays and for the opportunity to cater for the visiting American Navy. The life for the men of the British Navy in Wei Hai Wei was quite the opposite. Nothing to do except sports and the canteen on the island.

It was about this time that I was anxiously awaiting news from Sis about the arrival of our baby. She had bravely faced this event alone because when we decided to start a family she knew that it was most unlikely that I could be with her when her time came. It is the lot of sailors wives to face so much alone, In the period of which I speak there was so little compensation by way of salary, and holidays were the accepted two weeks a year. However I was soon to learn that Sis had given birth to a daughter at her parents' home at Kenton, Middlesex and of her christening some weeks later at the church at Harrow-on-the-Hill. She was called Patricia. Sis was truly a 'stout hearted lady'; all through her life she had to tackle so much on her own, which she did with calm and fortitude.

We returned to Shanghai and I was appointed to one of the oldest ships in the Customs fleet, the *C.P.S. Chuentiao.* Built in 1888 by Armstrong Mitchell and Co Ltd of Newcastle, England. She was 155 ft long with a 25 ft beam. She was a very comfortable old ship and spent a lot of her time moored fore and aft to her buoys in the Whangpoo River just opposite the Custom House.

To say the least of it Shanghai was a gay (in the sense the word was used in those days) town. There was a pretty full social life and as a newcomer and cousin of Douglas Murray, who was fairly senior in the Customs, I got a number of invitations from people in the Service. We were also expected to "call" on senior members and leave cards. The response to this was usually an invitation to dinner or a cocktail party. We single men usually went around in pairs and my particular friend of that time was "Ginny" Gilroy. Outside all this there were the cabarets and dance halls. Many of the "taxi" dance girls - so called because you paid to dance with them - were Russian. There was a large Russian population of "white" Russians in Shanghai. These people were Czarists and were called white as opposed to red (communist). They had escaped from Russia during the years of the revolution by going East with the retreating armies of the Czar, and had ended up in Siberia and crossed the border into China. Many of them said they were of Royal blood and it was a standing joke in Shanghai to talk about Russian Princesses. There were of course many Russians in Chinese border areas and at Harbin on the Siberian border where the Chinese customs had a station. They just moved into China and picked up life again there and moved down the coast and as far as India. Many of the men became policemen, or chauffeurs. The skilled ones became engineers, chefs, or hoteliers. They were a delightful people who accepted fate cheerfully. Some were employed in the C.M.C. and a number of our officers had Russian wives. Two red headed sisters Mitzi Glover and Valerie Cairns were both married to seagoing engineers in my department and both were friends of ours. These girls as children had come all the way from the Russian - Polish border to Eastern China ahead of the Bolsheviks.

During this visit to Shanghai, I was introduced to Ah Zung, our tailor. He was a good tailor and would come to the ship to give us fittings for new uniforms. He lived in his shop, as many did, and would cash cheques, or even lend money after hours when the banks were closed. He never grumbled, whatever time of night he was woken to cash a cheque. He even coped with cheques that "bounced" - he added them on to your monthly bill. Some years later my friend "Ginny" Gilroy gave an engagement party and the ring was proudly shown to another great friend of ours, Jim Skinner. Jim looked at the very nice ring and remarked "My!! that must have set Ah Zung back a bit." It was some time before he was forgiven.

My social life in Shanghai, which was fairly hectic, with a lot of new found friends was nearly the cause of my early demise. The River Whangpoo which runs through Shanghai and empties itself into the Yangtze at Woosung, on an ebb tide, runs fast and filthy. There are eddies and swirls round mooring buoys and the anchor chains of anchored vessels. It is said that if you fall in your chances of survival are poor.

I came back to the ship late one night, a cold night, dressed in a dinner jacket, overcoat, and hat. I got a sampan at the customs jetty to go the 200 yards or so to the *Chuentiao,* tied to her buoys in the middle of the river. I suppose I was fairly "happy". We got to the ship's gangway, I paid the sampan, stepped out and cold river water closed over me. When I surfaced I was some way downstream. The air trapped under my hat and coat brought me to the surface. The sampan man with great presence of mind had let go of the gangway and drifted down with the tide. When I surfaced the sampan was alongside and he hauled me aboard. Thank God he was a quick thinker. Next day my clothes were whistled off to the cleaners and the only people who knew about it were my steward and the Quartermaster, who was on gangway duty at the time.About the time I joined the Service the *Chuentiao* had been involved in a battle with a pirate junk in the Yangtze estuary. She was on a Customs patrol and sent her motor boat off to inspect a suspicious junk. The boarding party would have consisted of three or four armed sailors and an officer. In this case a young Norwegian officer named Kundrup. As soon as the boat got within range the junk opened up with rifle fire. Kundrup was killed and one of the sailors was wounded. The boat went smartly back to the ship. We were not police and were not interested in pirates. Had the junk not fired at the boat they would have been inspected, and if not smuggling would have been let go. This incident led to a lot of discussion about protective plating for the boats of the new fleet now under construction, the weight and inconvenience of which was to be a problem. Ignorance of the various types of junks may have led to this accident. Pirate junks were fairly obvious and we always left them alone if they were recognised as such. It was essential that one had a good knowledge of the types of junks usual in your district because it was a waste of time stopping every junk you saw. If a stranger appeared he was likely to be a smuggler.

My time in *Chuentiao,* old venerable and comfortable, had come to an end. It had been an interesting time of initiation into the Customs Service. I had met a lot of new people in Shanghai. Everyone wanted to know when my wife was going to come out from U.K. Each experience had been something new. Lighthouse tending in the *Chunhsing,* then anti-smuggling patrol in the mouth of the Yangtze in the *Chuentiao.* I had even seen a buoy changed. We picked up an overhauled light buoy from our yard at Pootung. With this hanging from the bow we proceeded out into the Yangtze and exchanged it for one needing overhaul which we then took back to Pootung yard. Today we talk about a 'learning curve'. I was certainly on a steep learning curve at that time and I had to make sure that I absorbed the experience because the next time I might have to do it. I would be the one in charge.

Chapter 6

NEW SHIPS - NEW PLACES
1933-1934

My next ship was to be the *Feihsing* under the command of Captain Lidwell, an ex Royal Navy Lieutenant Commander who had been in the Customs for some years. He was a bit pompous and had never done any preventive work before. We were to be stationed in Hong Kong.

Feihsing was under construction at Kiangnan Dock in Shanghai. The dockyard was some way up stream from the Customs House and to get there one had to travel through miles of slums in the Chinese part of the city. She was a twin-screw steamship about 175 feet long burning oil fuel. There were very comfortable quarters for the officers and the Captain, the latter had big day and sleeping cabins under the bridge.

The powers that be in the Customs had got the wind up after the attack on the *Chuentiao's* boat. So they ordered the bridge to be armour plated. This had the effect of making the ship a bit top heavy and though ballast had been added neither she nor her sister ship the *Huahsing* which I was later to command, were comfortable in bad weather.

Jim Skinner, who I had already met in Shanghai, was to be Chief Officer, and I was Second Officer and there was a Chinese 3rd Officer. Jim and I were to be great friends, and I am afraid Skinner and Briggs got a bad name for themselves owing to their riotous living. However, I don't think it could have been too bad because we both got quick promotion.After trials in Shanghai, the *Feihsing* was accepted and we sailed for Hong Kong, to add our weight to the Kowloon preventive fleet which consisted of one ship, the Likin, and a number of big steam launches.

The Chinese Customs had established three Customs Stations around the British Territory of HongKong. Samun was on the East and up the coast a few miles North of HongKong. Situated on a pretty island, there was a sheltered bay for junks to anchor. A good stream came down from the hill and from which we used to fill our fresh water tank. An office and houses for the staff completed the scene. There were about three foreign staff - the rest were Chinese. This station was strategically placed between Mirs Bay, mostly British territory, and Bias Bay which was Chinese. On the West, in the Canton delta, there was another Customs Station, Taishan, just outside British waters, it was staffed and organized similar to Samun. The third Customs station was at Sumchun. This was North of Kowloon where the railway crosses the border into China. The Sumchun River is the border between Hong Kong and China.

Our job was to patrol East of Hong Kong to make sure that all cargo junks called at the Samun station to pay their dues. Any cargo junks found evading the station were liable to seizure. There had been much smuggling from Hong Kong into China, and it was comparatively easy up to the present. It was planned that, together with the *Feihsing,* two more ships, now being built in Shanghai, would be added to the Kowloon Customs preventive fleet.

All goods imported into China now carried a heavy duty, so smuggling had become a very profitable industry. The popular goods to smuggle were everyday things such as sugar, piece goods (cotton materials), kerosene and so on. I remember one wet and rough night we caught a smuggler just outside Hong Kong waters, one man rowing a sampan with one bag of sugar. It seemed a shame to confiscate it. They were poor people and he could only afford to invest in one bag at a time. We seized his sugar and let him go. I expect he just went back for another bag. At this time there were only two 'watering holes' in Hong Kong that we frequented. One was the Hong Kong Hotel and the other the Peninsular. If you went into the former any day around 11 am you were sure to see someone you knew. Cash was not required, you merely signed a chit and forgot about it until the end of the month when the bill arrived. I am sorry to say that we all ran up enormous bills which it was a struggle to pay. Most of the young men tried to keep up a style for which thet were not adequately paid. This also applied to the Army and Navy. Though pay in the Customs Service was good the pay of Officers in the British forces at that time was woeful.

A group of us (Customs) might be sitting at a table in the lounge of the Hong Kong Hotel about 6 pm and a young army officer known to us would join the group. After enjoying a drink at the expense of whoever was "in the chair", he would suddenly remember he had a date and disappear with a polite "thank you". This we called "doing a Royal Scot". It happened that a battalion of the Royal Scots were stationed in Hong Kong at the time and we knew quite a few of them. This sometimes maligned - by us - regiment fought the Japanese in later years with great bravery and heavy casualties.

At this rate there was little chance of saving enough to pay the passage of my wife and baby daughter to Hong Kong. I was also paying my mother in law back the £72 she had put up to buy me out of the Admiralty service, and sending Sis more than I had been able to before. Various suggestions were made by my friends such as buying her a bicycle to ride across Europe and Siberia and into China. The only way I could see was through Seizure Money. The system was that any smuggled goods seized by one of our ships were sold and part of the proceeds of sale were allocated to the ship and divided in shares according to rank. This arrangement applied to all customs preventive staff, involved in a particular seizure, not only to the sea going staff. *Feihsing* up to the present had done no better than a few bags of sugar. This was not going to get my wife anywhere.

Fortune was soon to favour me. I had only been in the *Feihsing* for a couple of months when I was appointed to command the *Paktau* stationed at Swatow. This port is North of Hong Kong and is famed for its productions of lace and other needlework, and mandarin oranges. Paktau was a large seagoing steam launch and was a sister ship of the *Cheongkeng* shown in the photograph.

There is a thrill attached to one's first command even though it is small, and I joyfully took charge for the 24 hour run to Swatow. I reported to the Commissioner of Customs, a Mr Hughie Hilliard. A senior man, we were later to become great friends, to whom I am indebted for imparting some of his depth of knowledge of China and the Chinese Customs. Mrs Hilliard was in Britain at this time. The Deputy Commisioner was Mr.Edgar Bathurst. His wife was in Swatow.

Swatow was two or three miles up - river, the Bathursts lived on the town side, where the Customs House was, and the Commissioner had a lovely house across the river and also a bungalow down by the sea. It was a lovely setting, peaceful and quiet, everyone busy and the orchards flourishing. The great thing for me was that I was now in the area of the big smuggling from Japanese held Formosa, now Taiwan.

I was the only officer on *Paktau*. She had a Chinese coxswain, capable of taking the little ship to sea, who knew the district and quite a lot about smugglers. Previously the launch had gone to sea with one of the shore bound Customs men in charge and it was a new idea to hand these big launches over to the Marine Department.

I had a nice big cabin at the forward end but it was not much fun living on board while we were in port. Mr Hilliard came to the rescue and gave me a room in his lovely house. The house was large and cool with high ceilings and beautifully polished floors. The furniture was part Chinese antique and part European, also antique. The big dining room would seat about twenty people at a huge mahogany table. The furniture belonged to the C.M.C. but all the silver and linen was the property of the Hilliards. My bedroom opened on to an enclosed veranda with a tiled floor. There was no sanitation and I used a "thunder box", as a commode was called. My bath was a very large earthenware 'kong'. Standing about 4 foot high it was wide enough to squat in with the water almost up to your neck. In the morning, or as required, my kong was filled with warm water and a spare can of cold was also provided by the servant whose duty it was to look after me. You stepped up into your kong and stood or squatted. When finished you pulled out the plug and the bathwater ran out and down a drain in the corner. The 'thunder box' was emptied by the 'nightsoil' man in the small hours. I never saw or heard him. Nightsoil in China is a very valuable commodity and nothing is wasted. It all goes on the vegetable and fruit gardens

Sometimes we would only be at sea for the night and on return I could go and rest in the nice cool house - it was almost idyllic for me. I was my own man at last. I had the say, more or less, when I went to sea, where we patrolled, and what we did. My first taste of real responsibility and I accepted it joyfully.

It was not long before we made our first seizure, a medium sized junk early one morning. He had got becalmed and instead of being empty and well on the way back to Formosa he was stuck, still quite close to shore. The junk was loaded with sugar, piece goods, kerosene and sundries. An armed guard placed on board, sails lowered and a towrope passed and we proudly arrived in Swatow with our first seizure. The first faltering steps of Sis's journey to China.

The seizure we really wanted to make was a Japanese "puff-puff". These came from Formosa and were big wooden fishing boats with a single cylinder diesel engine. With a speed of six or seven knots they could make it to the coast from the 12 mile limit and back and unload in the hours of darkness. Being Japanese we had to be careful not to take them outside 12 miles and cause an incident. With Chinese junks it was a different matter. Any junk carrying a cargo of imported goods had to have a Customs clearance otherwise it was carrying contraband.

We got to know the favourite landing places and sometimes had information where and when a boat was due. The tactic for this was to leave port early and go in the opposite direction - then out to sea and out of sight. As soon as it was dark we would come back to the coast, lie off with no lights and the engines stopped, and listen. Everyone was on deck listening for the expected puff-puff-puff. It was quite unmistakable. Our steam engines were quiet and the smuggler could be heard until sighted. Then our lights were switched on, the searchlight switched on, and the "puff-puff" called upon to stop. A rifle shot was often sufficient but we had a 3 pounder gun as well with the crew "closed up". We seldom had to use the gun but a shot across the bow had an instant effect. An armed boarding party went off in our motor boat and if it was a smuggler they were told to proceed to Swatow, with us following.

The cargo and the boat were always forfeited and the crew left to find their own way back to Formosa. I think the boats were probably bought back at the auction as I never saw any in Chinese hands. We always wanted to find out where the smuggler was going, where he came from, and any other information we could extract. No one spoke Japanese and they did not speak Chinese. The answer was to write. There is sufficient similarity between Chinese and some

Japanese characters to be able to carry on a written dialogue. Usually with some result.

Our seizures were totting up and soon I had enough saved to send money to Sis for her passage. For some reason we were paid seizure money in cash and I remember having to go to the Bank with a great bundle of notes about $5,000.

We got in early one morning after a disappointing night of watching, waiting and listening for the puff-puff that never came. After completing my business at the Custom house I retired to the Commissioner's house for lunch and a rest. I was fast asleep, about three pm when I was called with a message from Bathurst, the Deputy Commissioner. The message was that information had been received that a puff-puff from Formosa was due that night in a certain little bay to the North of Swatow. The bay had a village behind the sandhills and it was a bay that we often kept an eye on. I sent a message off to the ship to say that we would go to sea again that night and that was that. I had a little more shut eye, went back to the ship, and we sailed just before dark. When out of the river we turned right and headed South down the coast towards Hong Kong. When it was quite dark we switched off all our lights and turned North to head for the rendezvous. It was a lovely night, with a calm sea, a slight swell and a light breeze off the land carrying all the scents of China; woodsmoke, fragrances, and the smell of lush vegetation.

Soon we got to where we wanted to be and with just enough way on to be able to steer we listened. The Coxswain listened, the crew listened, the engineer came up on deck to listen and I listened all the time. About midnight the Coxswain said "I think so puff-puff". I had heard it too. I stopped the engines and tried to decide where the sound was coming from. It seemed to be coming from our starboard quarter so I said "slow ahead hard a-starboard" and we turned slowly towards the sound. We were now heading South and the sound was right ahead and moving to the right. "Half ahead, 20 degrees starboard" and we moved to cut him off. "Full ahead"; a couple of minutes more, "Can see!!" said the coxswain and there was the luminosity of her bow wave and then the boat itself. We raced to cut her off. We switched on our lights, loaded the 3pdr. gun, opened the shutter of the searchlight and there she was, a fine Formosan fishing trawler, fully loaded and going flat out. I ordered 'Fire one round ahead'. Bang goes the 3pdr. and the puff-puff's bow wave dies away. 'Away motor boat'is the next order. The boat is quickly lowered, as we ease our own speed, and four armed sailors , ready by now with their rifles, jump down into the boat and head for our quarry. I take the ship to within about fifty yards and wait for our boat to come back. The boat returns leaving guards on the puff-puff. The report is that she is fully loaded with sugar, tins of kerosene, and bales of piece goods. I go to within hailing distance and tell our men to take her into Swatow and the ship will follow. An interested crowd turns out to watch and when I get to Bathurst's office later it is, "Well done Briggs that was a really good one". That made two and I was very pleased with what we had done in a few months.

My time in Swatow was soon to end, it had nearly ended earlier when I was staying at the Commissioner's seaside bungalow and got dumped by a breaker. My, that sand was hard, and I must have damaged a vertebrae in my neck because I have a lump to this day. The young recover quickly however, and after a night's rest I was better, but my sore neck lasted for days.My little ship was perhaps not much of a command and she might have got on all right without me. However, I brought new ideas and tried to smarten it up into a ship and not just a Customs launch. I don't think the coxswain really liked it because he had been used to running it his way. However we were making money and everyone was happy. My sojourn in *Paktau* lasted just long enough to pay for Sis's passage to China and to give her some travelling money. I was summoned to Shanghai to undergo an arms course.

Because the Customs was an armed service it was important that we knew how to handle the weapons provided and also knew enough to supervise the instruction of our own sailors. Therefore all sea going officers and senior sailors were sent to the Customs arms depot at Pootung yard for training. The Customs Armament Officer was Captain Lidwell, my Captain in the *Feihsing,* who had recently been given the job with an office in the Coast Inspectors Office in the Customs House. With the aid of a sergeant, kindly loaned, from the British Army battalion stationed in Shanghai, and a couple of senior Chinese sailors, already trained, we had quite an efficient set up.

Douglas Murray, who got me the Customs job in the first place, invited me to stay at his place for the period of the arms course which would take a month. He was not married and shared a house in the Shanghai Customs compound with another Customs man, Jack Storrs. A number of houses had been built in a group in a pleasant part of Shanghai to house European staff working either at the Customs House or the Inspectorate. The latter so called because the Inspector General and his staff had their headquarters there. The houses in the compound were large and roomy. A full staff was kept and household expenses were shared by whoever was living in the house at the time.

It was here I met Arthur Pittendrigh. He had been an Officer in Jardines shipping and had joined the C.M.C. about the same time as myself. Pitt, as everyone called him, became an instant friend and remained one until his sad death from cancer in Western Australia about 1968. There was a streak of the "playboy" in both of us and as Pitt was also staying in the house with us, it was easy to go out together. We spent the days at Pootung yard learning how to handle Lewis guns and 1/2 inch Vickers guns and of course rifles and pistols. The nights we spent in the night clubs and dance halls of Shanghai. It was often torture crossing the river to Pootung Yard with a blinding headache and a mouth like the bottom of a parrots cage. However we survived the month's course, passed with flying colours, and on completion I was appointed again to Hong Kong.

By now it was mid 1933 and the money I had made from customs seizures in Swatow was having its full effect. Sis with our baby daughter, Patricia, were on their way out from England on a P.& O. liner and were due to arrive in Hong Kong about the time I finished the arms course. However, travel up and down the coast was always by ship and was not very predictable to a day or so and it so happened that Sis arrived in Hong Kong a day before me. She was met by a bevy of friends of mine all unknown to her. Among them was Jim Skinner, who also became a lifelong friend until his death in the early 60's. They installed her safely in the Gloucester Building until my arrival next day.

We met again at last, just under two years after I left England to join *Belgol*. A joyous meeting with Sis, in blooming health in spite of sea sickness on the trip, and a 12 month old Patricia also blooming and just able to stand. I was shy of them both. Long separations create a gap, difficult to bridge even if a strong bond exists. One changes all the time, unnoticeable when living together but the cumulative effect while separated takes time to adjust to. A man has to shake off his recently resumed bachelor ways and again join a shared life and shared decisions. Selfishly I was inclined to cling and try to make the best of two worlds. In time it wore off and we were to settle down to a family life together over many years with only one other long and traumatic separation. Now we had to look around Hong Kong and find somewhere to live. Kowloon was usually cheaper than on the island and there was more acommodation available there too. So it was in Kowloon that we started our house hunting.

Chapter 7

THE GOOD LIFE

We moved from the Gloucester into a boarding house called the "Knutsford Hotel" in Kowloon and acquired an amah to look after Patricia. We had to look for somewhere permanent to live and as our own length of stay was never definite, it was usual to take over a flat or house from someone going on leave. This time we took over a flat in King Edward Road, Kowloon. I had to go on with my work and I had been appointed to a sea going launch named *Cheong Keng*. She was a sister ship to the Paktau that had been my first command in Swatow. We worked on a basis of ten days out and four days in port.

Members of the Chinese Maritime Customs service stationed in Hong Kong were in the position socially of being neither "flesh, fowl or good red herring". Our only ready made friends were our own staff. Hong Kong in those days was very British. The residents, were European, mostly Colonial Government staff, and the Armed Services (quite numerous in those days) with a busy Naval Dockyard and base. Then there were the many Europeans in the H.K. Police, including numerous "White Russians" who had escaped the revolution and gradually drifted down the coast from Manchuria. The big firms, Butterfield and Swire, Jardine Mathesons, Hong Kong and Shanghai Bank, Chartered Bank of India, Cable and Wireless, the oil companies, then the many smaller trading companies all had a number of employees from U.K.. There was a large indigenous European population of people born in Hong Kong and residing permanently there. There were also many Portuguese, mixed race, and Indian residents.

These formed the various strata of Hong Kong society into which we, who were quite transient, had to fit. We were eligible for the various clubs and we chose to belong to the Royal Hong Kong Golf Club and the U.S.R.C (United Services Recreation Club). Many of our friends were Service people, who were almost as transient as ourselves. Anyway we took to it like ducks to water. A visit to the lounge of the old Hong Kong Hotel would find us, if I was in port, at a table with some of our Customs or other friends.

In the evening the usual dinner dance would find us there again. The old hotel, called by its regulars "The Grips" was very much a meeting place where one was sure to see someone one knew.

In 1933 Hong Kong was one of the more delightful places to live. The cost of living was cheap, and servants were good and plentiful and also cheap. It is easy to entertain when all you have to do is tell the cook-boy "six people come dinner tonight". After discussing the menu he would go and purchase what was needed. Sis, who all her life had been very particular about her house, saw to the flowers and that would be that. A good cook-boy was always anxious that all went well. It often meant a job in the future with ones friends when you were transferred.

It was a roving life - you never expected to stay anywhere more than a couple of years and when told to transfer - you transferred. It is odd today that people grumble so much if they are transferred - the whole outlook on life, with house purchase mortgage and other commitments is quite different.

All was peace in 1933. There were only four first class hotels in Hong Kong in those days, the Hong Kong Hotel, the Peninsular, Gloucester Building and the Repulse Bay Hotel. The established custom in the Far East those days was the signing of "chits" for any service that was given in a hotel or a club. Once your credit was established you could sign a "chit" wherever you went. This was as dangerous as the plastic credit card of today and it was only too easy to run up a fantastic bill in the "Grips" (the Hong Kong Hotel) and then find difficulty in paying it.

Hong Kong was always crowded but it was not until the years 1937-39, when China was being overrun by the Japanese army, that refugees began to stream into the Colony. In those days there were no tunnels or underground railways. When you wanted to cross the harbour you took the Star Ferry, it cost 10 cents and took about ten minutes. Late at night, when the ferries had stopped running, you took a "walla -walla" motor boat from Blake pier or a sampan which though slower was cheaper. For the car owner there was a car ferry. This was very convenient if you lived in Kowloon and needed to go, say, to a dinner party at a house on the Peak. Transport was simple. Trams ran everywhere, though they were not much used by Europeans. There was and still is the Peak tram. A cable railway with two cars, one going up as the other comes down. There was a good road up to the Peak but steep with frightening hair pin bends. Rickshaws were used on the more level bits and you could go up to the middle levels in a sedan chair. Taxis were numerous.

It was the day of the open touring car and on a hot night it was the "done thing" to take a taxi round the island. The driver would put the hood and the windscreen down so the passengers got a cool blow. It was all fun. Swimming and picnics at Repulse Bay and Castle Peak, golf at Deepwater Bay and Fanling, tennis at the USRC, and dancing any night at the hotels, completed the picture. The cinema on Sunday night was quite an institution. No wonder that we all loved Hong Kong.

European residents of Hong Kong were usually smartly dressed. Men wore jackets and ties, the women mostly wore hats, and were always very smart. Slacks were not being worn at that time. We used to envy the Royal Navy who went about in an easy rig of shirts and shorts, long socks, shoulder straps denoted their rank - a rig worn in daytime only. While we men, had to contend with jackets, even though lightweight. Sis hated hats. When she had to, she wore large hats with great effect. We always went dancing in dinner jackets or white 'bum freezer' jackets, the women always wore long dresses.

We worked a lot from Samun Customs Station. This delightful island was situated between Mirs Bay (mostly British) and Bias Bay, Chinese. Smuggling junks and sampans would be out at night trying to cross the quite short distance from Mirs Bay round into Bias bay and we were kept busy looking for them during the dark hours. Thousands of wild ducks lived on Bias Bay and would stay quite still on the water, until the ship approached, and then rise in a cloud. It came to me that it might be possible to get duck for supper if we slowly crept up to them and then let fly with our Lewis Gun. We tried this one day but the ducks flew off, unscathed. Of course, I got very friendly with the Customs staff on the island and this is how we acquired a dog. One of the European staff at the Samun Customs station had a liver and white pointer called Nigger. This dog rather took to me and when the owner was being transferred he offered the dog to me, and I gladly accepted. Nigger settled in with the family and became one of the nicest dogs we ever had. He used to come to sea with me occasionally, and he loved walks and swimming.

I never seemed to stay long in one ship at that time and I was soon appointed to another big Customs launch called *C.P.S.Kuanlui*. She was built of wood and was used in the delta West of Hong Kong, an interesting area which took in Macau, the Portuguese territory across from Hong

Kong. Halfway between Hong Kong and Macau was an island called Lintin. It was virtually uninhabited except for some fishermen's huts. We often anchored there, watched the passing traffic, and I used to go ashore for a walk. At one time the island had been used as a base for the early English traders and their opium, before Hong Kong was established. I found an old abandoned graveyard with headstones still standing and the names of sailors and others who had died there. There were a number of women's names, and it must have been pretty grim there in those days and was probably malarial.

Macau was surrounded by flat country intersected by creeks and waterways. It was possible to enter these waterways by one entrance, cruise round and get out another way. Not that it did much good, but I felt it showed the Customs flag and was very interesting with all sorts goings on such as a 'duck boat'. These boats carried thousands of ducks who were moved from place to place and herded on and off the boat to feed in the wet paddy fields. On one of these trips we came out of our creek at an entrance that looked to me to be a bit shallow for us. I said to the Coxswain "Alright go out this way?." The reply was "Sometime can go sometime no can go". Very informative so I asked "Can go now?" The Coxswain replied, "I think so just now maybe can go!" Very reassuring, I'm sure, but we tried it and there were a couple bumps on the sand bar and we were over into deep water.

With all these waterways around Macau it was natural that there would be a lot of smuggling. The main means of transport for smugglers from Macau into this maze of creeks was by a type of boat we called a 'Snake boat'. They were long narrow boats paddled by six or so men. They were nearly always armed and would fight if they thought they could escape. It was quite usual for a Customs launch to return in the morning towing a couple of these boats with blood on some of the bags of sugar it had carried. We occasionally spent the night in one of these creeks but it was not our luck to get in a fight. We were fired on one night from the shore so we gave the spot where the firing seemed to come from a couple of bursts of Lewis gun and the firing stopped. We weighed anchor and moved to another spot.

The Customs were building up their fleet of patrol ships, which we foreigners had been engaged to take command of pending the training of suitable Chinese nationals. Only two had been completed to date and we were continuing to gain experience in customs work. Then I was appointed to command *C.P.S.Likin*. My rank was 2nd officer acting commander.

The Likin had been built in 1888 by Armstrong Mitchell and Co. Ltd of Newcastle so she was now 45 years old and in perfect condition. The masts for sails shown in the photograph had been removed. She was 135 feet long with a beam of 23 feet. The captain's cabin was quite luxurious. It was in the stern and rather like the stern gallery cabin one would have found in an old wooden battleship, beautifully fitted out in polished teak, comfortable chairs, a dining table, and a couple of square portholes facing aft. Quite the wrong place for a captain's cabin which should be somewhere under the navigating bridge. A ship's captain needs to be constantly available when called by the Officer of the watch. He should not have to walk all the way from the stern and up a couple of ladders to get to the bridge.

Some ships are lucky ships and some ships are happy ships. Like houses, especially old ones, they have what I can only call an influence. Some people are quite unaffected by it and others are. For me and for others *Likin* was an unlucky ship.

We had been sent for a three week trip to Hainan Island. There had been some smuggling into Hainan from the French port of Kwanchowan. The trip in itself was quite uneventful. We caught no smugglers but spent some time surveying a very nice sheltered bay we had found. It was

*C.P.S. Likin.
National Maritime
Museum photo.*

C.P.S. Cheongkeng. Paktau similar.

Author with 3 pounder gun.

shown on the chart but there no water depths given so we made a plan with the water depths shown and sent it off to our chart office in Shanghai. Surveying was one of the odd jobs that we were expected to do if opportunity offered. When we returned to Hong Kong at the end of the trip I found that Sis was in hospital with dysentery. She had been taken ill a few days before, and the amah had got the doctor who put her in an ambulance for the Canossa Hospital which was on one of the middle levels overlooking Hong Kong. I went to see her and she just knew it was me. Early next morning the phone rang - it was the hospital to tell me to come and say good-bye. They thought she was going but she had a good grip on life and after that day started to pick up. There was a shortage of emetine at that time in the colony, the one drug specifically used for dysentery at that time.

When Sis came out of the hospital she was pretty thin and groggy, and the lease of our flat was up. The people we rented it from were returning, so we moved. This time to a house belonging to H.K. Tramways. The employees who lived there had gone on six months leave. It was a very nice house, high up at Happy Valley, on the far side of the racecourse from Hong Kong. It was on a private road available only to the residents. The house was on two levels. All the underneath ground level part was servants' quarters and kitchens; the upper level was where we lived. A lovely deep cool veranda ran along the side that overlooked Happy Valley and all the exterior openings were covered with heavy folding steel grills, upstairs and down. Ostensibly very safe. Sis was very nervous when she came out of hospital so I left her one of the ships revolvers, an enormous .45 colt. She probably would not have been able to use it but it gave her some comfort as I had to go to sea again. It was a very nice house and we were there until we were sent to Shanghai after my term in *Likin*. At he end of our road there was a large sign saying NO ENTRY PRIVATE ROAD and our house was about 100 yards up the road. One night we came home in a taxi from Hong Kong in pouring rain and can it rain in Hong Kong. The taxi stopped at the sign." Go on up to the second house" says I. "You think me bloody fool" says taxi driver!. So that was that, we walked the rest of the way and got soaked. I don't blame the driver. If he had been reported he would have lost his taxi licence and his livelihood.

We continued the routine of ten days at sea and four days in port. When in port we used to anchor in a quiet area off Wanchai just East of the Naval dockyard. The other Customs launches used to anchor there too. It was possible to get close enough, to the steps, for me to be seen from the ship and a boat would be sent to take me off to the ship.

The ships were kept spotless and discipline was strict - inasmuch as the days routine was strictly adhered to. Men on duty in port such as boats' crews, quartermasters and officers of the day always wore uniform. Sunday Divisions began with a full inspection of the crew and the ship. It kept everyone on their toes and one had to search to find something at fault. One Sunday I was inspecting the crews quarters and there was a sweet little black puppy about six months old tied up outside the galley. I turned to the Boatswain and asked him whose dog it was. The reply shook me a bit. "Dog belong cooks, bymebye make chow". Poor little black dog. I never saw it again. All the time I was in Customs ships I never had any trouble with the crew. They were hard working, obedient and good humoured. Their idea of what is funny was sometimes unusual. One of the sailors lifted an ammunition box off a .5" machine gun and then dropped it on his toe. He was in agony but the others thought it a huge joke. He had to be sent ashore to the doctor.

It was usual when cruising off the coast at night to switch off our navigation lights. This was reasonably safe because we were too close to the coast to be in the regular shipping lanes and it gave one a chance to see a smuggling junk or sampan before they saw you. We also steamed at slow or half speed which made it safer still but it did mean that the officer of the watch on the bridge and the lookout man forward had to be very alert. Under these circumstances I did not always stay on the bridge but often dozed in an armchair in my cabin.

One night, just on midnight, when we were steaming without lights there was a sudden commotion and I rushed up to the bridge to find that we had collided with one of the big Hong Kong fishing junks. We picked up about four people who had been on deck but the rest of the family and crew, ten in all, had been asleep and were trapped in the upturned hull. We did what we could. We managed to get some bodies before the upside down junk slowly sank. It was a most distressing situation and I sent a radio signal to the Commissioner of Chinese Customs (my boss) in H.K.; the message read "Sunk junk 10 dead - Briggs" and returned to port. We were met by a police launch in H.K. They asked me, and the Second Officer who had been in charge of the watch, what had happened and took away the bodies and the survivors. The police had no further interest as the accident happened outside H.K. territorial waters and we were a Chinese Government vessel. However, we had an inquiry in the Commissioner's Office and the incident was regarded as an accident. I presume the the situation was that the Second Officer had come on the bridge for his midnight to 4 am watch just on midnight. The 3rd officer handed over but obviously had not waited long enough for the 2nd officers eyes to get used to the darkness. At least that is how I explained it to myself. This particular Second Officer held a British Extra master's certificate. He was very clever but as a seaman, he was not very efficient. It was a sad accident. Perhaps I should have been on the bridge at the time the watch was handed over, but this should not have been necessary. The captain is always finally responsible and this incident has been on my conscience over the years. It could well be put down to inexperience. It should have been in my 'night order book' that I was to be called at the change of the watch. A night order book contains the Captain's instructions, navigational and other, for what should occur during the night. The officer coming on duty reads and signs the orders before taking over the watch and it is usual to include the words "Call me if.........".

We were on patrol outside Hong Kong when we received a message to say the *U.S.S.Fulton* was on fire, some miles up the coast. *Fulton* was a rather old American warship which had spent many years on the China station, showing the flag, and was a regular visitor to Hong Kong. By the time we got to her position it was getting dark; she was well on fire and the crew had already been taken off. There was great danger of an explosion and we kept guard on her all night warning various passing ships to keep away. Soon after daylight another U.S. ship arrived on the scene and we went on with our patrol. Some months later I was thrilled to receive a quite magnificent parchment certificate, from the Chinese Government, mostly written in Chinese and covered with red seals,commending me for our action, and expressing the gratitude of the American Government. Unfortunately this fine document, of which I was quite proud, was left hanging on the wall of our flat when the Japanese captured Hong Kong in late 1941.

All went well until I received orders that I was to take over a new ship, now completing in Shanghai. It would be a month or more before the ship was ready to be handed over. The end of my time in *Likin* had come. My instructiona were that the whole family was to go to Shanghai.

I was ashore and my steward was packing up the few belongings I kept on board when he found the .32 calibre automatic pistol which belonged to me. I kept it in the drawer of my desk with a magazine in the butt but not pushed home and no round in the breech. My steward had evidently not seen it before so he called the Chief Officer to ask if it belonged to me or to the ship. The Chief officer picked it up, pushed the magazine fully home, cocked it, thereby putting a round in the breech, and with his left hand over the muzzle pulled the trigger and shot himself through the hand. Almost unbelievable but it happened. Fortunately the bullet had gone through his hand without doing any damage. For me *Likin* was an unlucky ship as it had been for others, but not all. First my wife's close brush with death when she had dysentery, then the junk accident, and finally the stupid incident with my pistol.

So it was off to Shanghai in one of Butterfield and Swires steamers, an old friend Sid Barling in command. Sis is the world's worst sailor and Sid suggested she went to bed and he would send some onion soup to her cabin. This was a very special soup made by his cook. Of course the results were disastrous!! The soup went down the washbasin.

Accommodation had been arranged for us in a very nice residential hotel so Sis, Patricia, and the amah settled in. I went daily to see my new command *C.P.S. Soohsing,* being finished off in Kiangnan Dockyard, some way up river on the outskirts of Shanghai.

It was the first time Sis and I had been in Shanghai together and we made the best of every minute of it. Then, Shanghai was a very social place. Not only from a point the view of gaiety and entertainment, but also from the point of view of getting to know our senior people and of them getting to know us. Sis's cousin, Douglas Murray, who was in Shanghai was able to introduce us to various friends of his.

The head of the Marine Department was Louis Carrel and his wife Lucy. He was the Coast Inspector and his domain covered everything to do with the whole length of the China coast and the great Yangtze River. He was assisted by two deputy Coast Inspectors, an Armament Officer, another European in charge of the chart depot, a European male secretary, and typists and messengers. On the opposite side of the Whangpu river was our Pootung buoy yard. A number of technical men were employed here including a Japanese diver, a very charming man who I got to know fairly well. The Pootung yard was a busy place where all navigational and mooring buoys were kept and overhauled. The large workshop also cared for the machinery for the various lighthouses. Lighthouses being one of our major responsibilities. All the lighthouses on the China coast, in those days were manned. So all the light keepers were members of our staff, together with lights mechanics and lighthouse engineers. The foreign staff came from almost every country in the world. British were possibly in the majority then came the Scandinavians, also a seafaring race, and Japanese of course though not very many of them. The month or so that we were in Shanghai was a marvellous introduction to all the people that mattered and this was to stand me in good stead for my career in the Chinese Customs.

The day came when *C.P.S. Soohsing* was ready for trials - a great thrill. I had never been in command of a brand new ship before. The trials were run by the builders and I had nothing to do except stand on the bridge and watch what was going on. All went well with the trials. The two big diesel engines ran perfectly, as did all the other machinery. Everything was electric - the steering, the capstan for raising the anchor, and the after docking winch. A few days later we set sail for Hong Kong, Sis and Patricia returned by coastal steamer. I was very proud of 'Sister Soosy', as I called her.

Soohsing was built to operate in the shallow waters of the Canton delta. That is West of Hong Kong over to and around Macau and North and South of this line. The smugglers came from H.K. and Macau and used any type of craft. The ship was driven by twin M.A.N. diesel engines and was of very shallow draft - about six feet. The speed was supposed to be 15 knots when required but this was very seldom used. It was discovered early in our operations that the design of the big end bearings was faulty. The bearing surface was insufficient for the 600 H.P.

C.P.S. Feihsing
Huahsing similar

Hong Kong Harbour looking down on Naval Yard.
Tamar under white roof.

C.P.S. Soohsing.

each engine developed and if the engines were run at full speed the white metal in the bearings collapsed. The MAN engineers came to us again and again and tried many kinds of metal. The problem was insoluble so we eventually made it a rule not to exceed 12 knots except for a few minutes.

Sis and I found a very nice first floor flat at Pokfullam. The flat was in a group of buildings owned by Mrs Weil. She was a rich old lady - who owned Sennet Freres the jewellers and had many other interests. She also had four Australian terriers. Our old pointer, Nigger, hated small dogs and taking him out, except in the car, was always a trial because the moment we got near Mrs.Weil's house all the little dogs rushed out and attacked him.

The time in *Soohsing* was uneventful and very pleasant. Most of our work was done at night and we would anchor in a quiet little bay during the day and swim when the weather was warm.

My Chief Engineer, Jimmy Steele, suffered from chronic seasickness. Owing to the shallow draft the ship was very lively in rough weather. Poor Jimmy would come on to the bridge and say "Could we shelter somewhere, I have had enough of this?" So I would say to myself - "its too rough for small smugglers tonight" and head for a sheltered anchorage.

We must have had a very routine time with *Soohsing* because my memories are mostly of the very nice flat at Pokfullam and our social life in Hong Kong. Patricia was growing rapidly and was about four years old by now. A delightful and smiling child who was never any trouble. Our amah, Ah Koi, who had started as a non English speaking wash amah was now Patricia's amah with a good command of English. She was a charming and intelligent woman whose home was at Shek Lung between Hong Kong and Canton. We had acquired, some time ago, a companion for Nigger. A beautiful liver and white pointer called Sue. I used to take them to sea with me in, turn.

I kept my 12 gauge shotgun on board the ship and often used to land when out on patrol and take a walk through the paddy (rice) fields and small farms. With one of the pointers it was often possible to bag a quail, a snipe, or a pigeon. Looking back I wonder how safe I was alone on these walks but the people I met were always friendly and smiling so that I got no impression of danger.

Our routine of 10 days out and four days in port gave me plenty of time at home. There are happy recollections of sitting on the enclosed veranda of our flat, with an evening drink, and watching the setting sun over Lamma Island. There was a lovely view of blue sea and the movement of junks and small craft. We have never lived with as nice a view before or since. I remember meetings with friends at the Hong Kong Hotel and the occasional dinner dance, and as we both loved dancing we made the best of every opportunity.

It was towards the end of my time in command of *Soohsing* that I started to get nervous. Maybe I needed a holiday, maybe it was some kind of throwback to the serious accident with the junk when I had *Likin*. I did not seem to mind leaving harbour, I had then had a few days rest, but the day we were due to return from patrol I would develop this feeling of foreboding. We used to enter Hong Kong from the East and go right through the harbour to anchor in Kowloon Bay. Sometimes on the way in we would call at the oil depot on Stonecutters Island for fuel, making the harbour trip a bit longer. The harbour was as crowded then as it is today; junks and sampans sailing and rowing in all directions; the cross harbour ferries, big ships, little ships and the Royal Navy tied up to their buoys. I was perfectly all right at sea - it was just a thing about the crowded harbour. I am sure I am not the only shipmaster who gets the jitters now and again. We almost never had local leave - unless sick leave. I did not have the faith that I have today. In those days I had not realized the power of prayer to remove fear. Now I would unhesitatingly ask God to remove my fears. It always works.

Suddenly, quite unexpected and out of the blue, came word that I was to be appointed to the Coast Inspectors Office in Shanghai. I must have made a good impression or should I say "we" while in Shanghai the year before. Our transfer was to take place in October and I was to be in charge of the Armament Office while the present Armament Officer, Captain Lidwell, went on a years leave. Eventually the whole family Sis, Patricia, Ah Koi and Nigger embarked on a coastal steamer for Shanghai. I gave Sue to the Captain of *H.M.S. Moth,* a river gunboat stationed in the Canton delta (West River). We often found ourselves anchored in the same cosy spot; we visited each others ships and became very friendly. He gave me a delightful watercolour of his ship which I lost during the war. We couldn't manage two dogs and I couldn't part with Nigger.

Chapter 8

A YEAR IN SHANGHAI

It was sad in a way leaving our nice first floor flat at Pokfulam with the lovely view. We had been so happy there. Patricia growing up - Sue with her nine puppies and the friendly Weil family as neighbours and landlords. There are no views in Shanghai.

We all packed into a taxi to go to the ship and offered the cook a lift into Hong Kong which he accepted. He had been a good cook and we had got on well except that he did occasionally come back at night a bit under the weather. At his request we dropped him off in H.K. and when I said goodbye I added the admonition "more better in next job you no drink so much!!".

The trip to Shanghai on a coastal steamer was uneventful and on arrival I found that a service apartment had been arranged for us until we found a flat or house and we were warmly welcomed by our friends. Our first visitor was Sis's cousin Douglas Murray. I offered him a gin, poured it out and added the correct quantity of water. After saying "Cheerio" we drank. Mine seemed a bit weak so I said "is yours O.K.?" His was weak too. I looked at the bottle - it had been well watered and barely tasted of gin - cook had the last laugh.

When we opened one of our trunks it contained yards and yards of highly dutiable cotton fabric. Sis said to Ah Koi "what is this?" "Belong my" says Ah Koi.
"You could have got us into big trouble".
"No trouble - Customs men never open master's boxes".
Of course she was quite right - we had come ashore in great style and no questions asked. The Armament Officer had an office on the Marine Department floor of the Custom House. The present incumbent was a Lieutenant Commander Lidwell RN (retired). I knew him fairly well because he had been in command of the *Feihsing,* one of the first of the ships of our building program to which I had been appointed Second Officer soon after I joined the Customs.

Lidwell was due for leave and I, who had never worked in an office before, was to take over from him until he returned a year later. He was a particularly fussy individual and everything in the office was organised - his way. We had a few days to hand over and soon my head was filled with loads of information and detail of how he did this and that. It was not long after he left that things began to be done "my way". I got the feeling that he thought it rather an indignity to have to hand over to such a junior as myself. His rank was Commander and I was still a Second Officer.

The responsibilities of the office were mainly routine, and included the training courses in the use of arms for our marine officers, senior seamen, and outdoor staff who manned the various Customs stations round the coast. There was at that time a British regiment stationed in the International Settlement of Shanghai. One of the contributions they made was to lend us a sergeant as instructor for our arms course. I used to go over to Pootung yard two of three times a week to watch what went on. The repair and replacement of weapons, the ordering and the budgeting for next year were also on my plate together with making sure each successive training class was filled.

This was all simple enough and largely a matter of routine. It just needed keeping an eye on to see that it ran smoothly. It was the odd jobs that I found difficult to do. If there was a sudden panic and a report had to be written the Coast Inspector would say "Oh, Briggs can do that". So poor old Briggs became the receptacle of all sorts of problems. It even devolved on me to write the "Report of the Marine Department" Chinese Maritime Customs 1936." From all over China and up the Yangtze river voluminous reports and statistics would arrive on my desk. From these I made up the report, in the form of a book with yellow paper covers, which was sent to Chinese Consuls and Embassies all over the world. In fact it was a Chinese Government publication. Never having done anything of this kind before I found it very challenging but incredibly interesting.

We soon found a flat in the French concession. We talked ourselves into getting a car, an "A" model Ford two seater - we could usually justify to ourselves anything that we really wanted. It was quite a way from our flat to the Custom House but with a car I was able to come home to lunch - of the savings that justified the car. Shanghai police were very strict about driver's licences and would not accept U.K. or H.K. licences so we both had to pass a test

There was a big undercroft garage under the Custom House where we could park, and Hankow Road ended opposite the back entrance and the garage. Also this particular road changed its one way direction so as to go down town in the morning and uptown in the afternoon. Traffic was very heavy there were rickshaws, bicycles, handcarts, pedestrians, and hawkers and food sellers had sequestered areas for themselves on the edge of the pavement. Accidents were surprisingly few, but the noise of horns and voices was ear splitting. Sis once got entangled with a rickshaw without much damage to either. Another time on the way home I had to stop suddenly and " crash" a cyclist, who must have been going flat out, hit the back of the car and landed spreadeagled on the roof. The car was undamaged but the bicycle was a bit bent and the rider bruised.

Senior Staff of the CMC lived in a suitable style and a certain amount of luxury, though extravagance was unheard of. Luxury fifty years ago meant comfort and servants, luxury today seems unbelievably extravagant, and people are so much less relaxed with little time to enjoy it.

The Coast inspector and his wife, Louis and Lucy Carrel lived in a very nice comfortable house (75 Route Ferguson) in the French concession. We had many delightful dinners with them and drinks on the lawn. Vodka and black caviar being a favourite and no one ever seemed to worry about driving home. Vodka is a bit of an acquired taste. The best way to take it is neat and take a bite of something immediately after each sip. This is where caviar comes in.

The highlight of our year was dinner with the Inspector General of Customs. Sir Frederick and Lady Maze were figures of whom we, at our age and seniority, stood rather in awe. Sir Frederick was English but Lady Maze was Australian. They were warm and friendly people who made their junior guests, such as ourselves, feel relaxed and at home. The guests were carefully chosen so that ranks were compatible.

Dinner was of course very black tie. Drinks before hand, served by the I.G.'s servants dressed in white and trousers tied with black at the ankles and black Chinese shoes. Round black silk caps, red cummerbunds, and white gloves completed the outfits. The same that would have been worn before the revolution, except that in those days all would have had pigtails.

The "calling" system was still in vogue in those days and Sis, as the newcomer, was expected to call and leave cards on senior people. This was later rewarded by an invitation to dinner or cocktails. One of the favourite ways of entertaining was Sunday night dinner and after dinner the host and hostess took their guests to a cinema. After the show was over the younger ones often finished up in one of the Shanghai night clubs of which there were many. Monday morning in the office was sometimes pretty dreary.

The system of renting houses or flats of people who were on leave meant that often one's longest tenure of an establishment was six months. We had to move from the flat half way through our year in Shanghai and found a very nice two storey house off Yu Yuen Road. I think the mosquitoes were the worst feature. The house had screens on the downstairs windows but not on the first floor. We hated mosquito nets - they add to the heat. So we had to suffer the mossies instead. In summer Shanghai is hot, often reaching to 100 F or more in the day. However at night as a great concession - it would go down to 98 F or so. This was the worst part of it. Shanghai was too far inland to be affected by the sea or sea breezes. It was also very flat and during the cyclone (typhoon) season a high tide would back up all the storm water drains for a long way inland making everything very unpleasant. The Custom House had been built on a raft, a system used when the soil is too deep for piles, and over the years it had sunk slightly below the level of the Bund. Whenever there was a flood the Custom House stood in the centre of a small lake. Wooden duck boards led to the front but the garage was flooded.

Winter of course was a different matter. Not much snow but a lot of frost. I remember once Ah Koi had left some wet towels on the line overnight, in the morning she came running in "Look missie, look missie"! The towels were as stiff as boards. Being Cantonese and from the South she had never seen anything like that before.

The great experience of our year in Shanghai was making friends and getting to know the Customs staff, not only in our own Marine Department but also the indoor staff. I should explain that the indoor staff were those who worked solely in the various offices and included the Marine Department and sea going officers at that level. The outdoor staff were the hard workers who manned Customs Stations, searched steamers and junks, dealt with passengers baggage and so on. Between the two came the appraisers and valuers who dealt with the levying of duty on incoming cargoes. In Shanghai the various grades kept to themselves, but in the smaller ports we all knew each other and your rank made no difference. There was a social dividing line between indoor staff and outdoor staff. Among those we made friends with were Isla and "T.D." Corfield. He was a very senior member of the River Staff★ and had an office in the Customs House to deal with the affairs of the river. They were great friends of the Carrels and took us juniors under their wing. Isla was much younger than her husband. She was tall and dark, danced like a dream, and liked younger men. She was quite the life and soul of any party.

Coast staff and River Staff were not up to that time interchangeable. The European coast staff had masters' certificates, but this was not necessary for the river launches and the surveying and conservancy work that was called for. However Louis Carrel felt that some of us could interchange and Sis and I were promised that after our home leave - due soon - that we would be sent up the Yangtze. Sadly, and thanks to the Japanese, this never happened.

Things were done differently in Shanghai and a little care was needed so as not to upset one's servants. Our cook-boy used to do the shopping at a store nearby and at the end of the first month the store sent an account which Sis paid by cheque the next time she passed. A few days later a very disappointed "boy" came and complained the storekeeper would not give him his "cumshaw" as missy had paid the bill. In future he was given the cheque and got his percentage from the storekeeper.

Soon after we settled in there seemed to be a lot of noise, late at night, in the kitchen. So I went in to see our cook. There was a strange man, with two or three large pots, cooking merrily

★ Yanztze River

on our stove. In reply to my request "What thing?" I was informed "my brother has street food stall and cook for tomorrow!!!" It never happened again - at least to my knowledge, after what I said!!

We were of course always hard up. Though well paid it did not go far with our very gay social life. and we had to return the many invitations we received. The easiest and least expensive way was to give a cocktail party. Vodka was then Shanghai $1.50 a bottle about two shillings or 20 cents Australian today and mixed with fruit juice it "made" the party. Of course other drinks were available if required. It was easy to get staff and crockery and glasses because your "boy" enlisted the help of your friends' "boys" and they came and brought extra glasses as required. As a visitor to a party you might well be served with one of your own glasses. Should you wish to give a dinner party, one of the easy way was to call in the Japanese.

There were a number of Japanese caterers to choose from. All you had to do was move the furniture out of the dining room. Two or three young Japanese women arrived in a van and set up a large round table in your dining room with cushions to sit on. They brought all the food and the saki which they cooked on the table with a charcoal brazier. It was quite inexpensive and all the hosts had to do was move the furniture and pay the bill.

Customs staff were given full medical attention. Local doctors groups entered into a contract with the Customs and we had to nominate which group of doctors we chose. Sis was advised to have a fairly large operation during our time in Shanghai. This was arranged for the best hospital in Shanghai and the night before Sis had to go in we went out with our friends on a real party. In the early hours at a cabaret we visited we saw one of our doctors very much under the weather. This was Dr R..... He was well known for leading a fairly wild life. Anyway the next day, or I suppose the day after the operation took place and when Sis was recovering we asked who had done the operation. The reply was Dr R... However, later in England Sis was examined by my Aunt, Dr Ethel Vaughan-Sawyer who said "I could not have done it better myself". So all was well, but it was some cause for worry until we got a good report.

All this time we had our dear old dog Nigger with us. He was a playmate for Patricia who could dress him up in dolls clothes and he never minded. Big dogs for little children. Nigger was big and strong and knew he could just walk away if he got tired of what Patricia wanted to do. However he hated little dogs. Memories of Mrs Weil's Aussie terriers. One day I left the flat to take him for a walk, unfortunately not on his lead, and we met a Chinese lady from another flat with a Peke - also not on a lead - Nigger dashed at it and picked it up in his mouth. Fortunately I managed to rescue it and many apologies and all was well but the lesson about small dogs was remembered.

Looking back on it all I realise how we wasted our chance to really get to know and understand the very likeable Chinese people. We did not even make a point of enjoying the wonderful food of the different regions in which we lived. We were young and gay and enjoyed a good time with people we knew and liked, the European community, that way was the easy way and required no effort on our part. In those days it was not the done thing to mix with the Chinese. We worked with them, I had Chinese both senior and junior to me, and we were friendly but did not mix socially. People of mixed race were not really accepted by the Europeans or the Chinese for that matter. It was sad because we had such a marvellous opportunity to really absorb much of what is so fine about China - certainly the Old China. One of our officers was married to a mixed race Japanese. She was a delightful lady, well educated and efficient. We used to say what a good mixture Japanese and English made.

Nigger was a dear dog but he did have a capacity to get himself and us into trouble. One Sunday we thought it would be nice to take him for a good walk in the country. At this time the countryside was peaceful, Chiang Kai Shek and the Kuomintang government was in full control. So off we went in the car through the city and out into the country, far away from the international concessions. The country is very flat, and on the Yangtze River flood plain are mainly vegetable gardens to supply the city of Shanghai with its population of millions. The area is divided up with wide grassy paths to make transport easier to and from the garden areas. Domestic animals such as the occasional water buffalo or goat are tethered so as to make use of the grass on the pathways. You learn to keep well clear of the buffalo. They hate the smell of Europeans and will attack if you get too close, yet a little Chinese boy can ride on their backs to bring them in at night. All was well this lovely Sunday afternoon, hardly anyone in sight, and we could see a little group of Chinese village houses some distance away. Off we went on our walk and before long we met a tethered goat. Nigger decided he didn't like goats, the goat did not like dogs either and tried to butt Nigger. There was some barking, shouts at Nigger from me. Nigger got hold of the goat and I managed to pull him off. Then we found ourselves surrounded by villagers shouting and gesticulating angrily. We could not understand what they said but it was obvious we were accused of hurting the goat and they wanted compensation. One man held me by the lapels of my jacket to try and keep us there. We seemed to be involved in an impasse and at a loss to know what to do next. No one spoke any English and everyone was angry. By some miracle a European couple, Mr. and Mrs.Gompertz arrived - they had seen the confrontation from their house some 1/4 mile or more away. Were we glad to see them. They spoke Chinese and succeeded in calming the shouting villagers and found out who owned the goat. There seemed to be no injury to the goat, though the owner said there was. However, he finally admitted that the goat seemed O.K. It was decided that next Sunday we would all meet at the Compertz house, the goat would be inspected and if any injuries had developed - compensation would be paid. Fortunately the Gompertz were well known and obviously trusted by the villagers who all went off peacefully. However that was the end of our walk and we went home to return again next Sunday.

The appointed day arrived and off we went to the Gompertz home. We stayed all afternoon being given tea and other refreshments. However no goat and no villagers turned up so all was well. We thanked the Gompertz for their trouble - I don't know what would have happened without their intervention. We would have had to produce money and we never carried much with us anyway.

Chinese have a great sense of humour and a story is told similar to ours where a foreigner's dog bit a pig on the tail while out for a walk. The usual crowd collected and demanded payment for the pig. The foreigner who could speak Chinese asked how much pig meat was worth and was told 60 cents a catty (750 grams). The foreigner thought for a while then he said "one pigs tail say 1/4 catty - I will pay you 15 cents". This novel approach amused the crowd so much that everyone burst out laughing and the red faced pig owner had to accept his 15 cents. Humour will get you a long way in China, but you do need to speak the rather difficult language.

Our time in Shanghai was drawing to a close and unfortunately poor Nigger developed heart worms. The eggs of these worms are mosquito borne and the worms develop in the bloodstream, finally killing the dog. The vet gave him an injection to kill the worms and he said "if the dog survives he will be pretty sick for a while. He will get pneumonia so keep him warm." We did. Sis made a coat for him as it was now October and getting cold in North China. Nigger was very ill for a while but eventually recovered - he was a lion-hearted old dog.

This last year was possibly the most rewarding of any year. I had learnt a lot about office work and how a big office was organised; I had pleased the Coast Inspector who had selected me for the job; and we met many of the senior people in the indoor staff of the Chinese Maritime Customs. We were in a period of history where your wife could be an important asset, or alternately a hindrance. If you were employed by one of the big British companies or Banks in India or the Far East it was important that your wife was socially accepted. Should a young bank employee decide to marry a girl of mixed blood, he would be given the choice, call it off or face the sack. Regional accents were not acceptable either, and how you spoke and behaved socially were important to your chances of promotion. We both spoke with no accent even though neither of us had had a very good education but we came from educated people who spoke well and read a lot. Sis was tall, good looking with dark red hair. She was elegant with a good dress sense and a sense of colour. She ran a well ordered home and any social graces came from being brought up in an army officers family. To my dear Sis I owe much, and a good portion of my success, while in the Chinese Customs, can be attributed to her dignity, bearing, and friendly nature. In China you needed to play either bridge, or mah-jong. Sis played the latter and this was all part of the social round.

Lidwell was due to return from leave by 15th. October 1936 and I was officially informed that I was promoted to Acting Commander and appointed to command the *C.P.S. Huahsing* stationed at Chefoo. Together with word of my new appointment I received the nicest letter I have ever had, from Louis Carrel, the Coast Inspector, thanking me for my year on his staff. (see appendix IV)

The first thing to do was to get in some Japanese packers. Though we lived in furnished houses all our linen, cutlery, crockery, had to be carted around with us. Quite an undertaking when two years was regarded as long enough in one place. The packers arrived with bales of straw and proceeded to make neat packages of each breakable item. The item was then thrown across the room on to the growing pile. It was certainly a bulky way of packing but very effective. We had collected a lot of extra stuff recently. It was a period when the Japanese had started making consumer goods for export and a trip to one of the big Japanese stores in Hongkew (the Japanese concession area) revealed an amazing array of glassware and other homeware at amazingly low prices. So we stocked up on many items.

When all was ready, and after days of goodbye parties with our many friends, we left for Chefoo on theButterfield & Swire ship *S.S. Shuntien*. Patricia, now four, Ah Koi, our delightful amah, and Nigger, our old pointer dog wrapped up in his pneumonia jacket. We were warmly greeted in Chefoo and a house had been found for us. Wherever we went there was friendship and by now we were getting fairly well known. It is a most enjoyable experience to go to a strange place and be greeted with a warm welcome; to find a house and servants all ready for you; and as soon as you have settled invitations and visitors begin to arrive. There was a great warmth among the staff of the CMC which I will never forget.

Chapter 9

NORTH CHINA AND NIPPON
1937 - 1938

Chefoo is now called Yentai again. The name Chefoo belongs to a tiny fishing village on the harbour side of the bluff. It is in Shantung province and faces North across the Pohai Gulf towards Korea. At that time Korea was a colony of Japan and a lot of smuggling into China from Korea had taken place. By the time we got to Chefoo the smuggling had almost ceased, Entirely due to the activities of the Customs Cruisers.

Before the arrival of Europeans Chefoo was a small fishing village but in 1858 it became a "Treaty Port" under a treaty with China. Foreigners were permitted to carry on trade with anyone and move about freely and come and go with their merchandise. Then came the white businessmen, merchants, traders, sailors and of course missionaries. By 1860 the place was a busy thriving port, and the foreigners revived some of the traditional industry such as silk weaving.

The port is dominated by the Bluff, which was connected to the mainland by a level spit of land. On the Western side a long curving breakwater had been constructed which enclosed a very safe and comfortable harbour. My ship had its own mooring buoy which was always free when we returned to harbour. To the East of the Bluff stretched a beautiful beach of white sand and most of the town faced this beach. A sea wall had been constructed with a narrow roadway in front of the houses. This was the shortest way for us by bicycle or rickshaw into the town area.

We moved into our nice house but we were told it was not permanent and we would have to move as soon as its owners returned - which was quite usual. The weather was now getting cold and stoves of the, pot belly variety, were brought out and fires lit. We used coal for heating and such good coal it was too. It came from the huge mines near the Manchurian border.

The Customs staff consisted of: the Commissioner, B.F.(Dick) Foster-Hall and his wife Ronnie, the area Commander, Ian MacRobert (whom we knew well). The Danish Harbourmaster, Strandvig and his wife, a talented lady with two dear little boys about the same age as Patricia. The boys were called Torbin and Eppa. It was a most disciplined family and after a meal the boys bowed to their mother and thanked her for the meal.

Dick and Ronnie Foster-Hall were a delightful couple. She was a petite person and a red head as was Sis. She was going grey and used to say I am a real redhead - I'll prove it if you like!! There were some other European Customs staff, and as we were a small community we got to know each other well and on the appropriate occasions there would be children's parties and adult parties in the Customs Club.

Ian MacRobert, who was the Area Commander, was my direct boss and was responsible to the Commissioner for the running of the ships. He would pass on to me the instructions for each voyage - where to go, what to look for and how long to be away, usually 10-20 days. Ian had been in Hong Kong when we were there and had married a widow in Hong Kong, whom we knew. After a couple of years Ian's wife died in Canton, under circumstances I believe were tragic. Ian was what the Scots call 'Fey'. People who seem to be in touch, very often, with the spirit world. Such people have the capacity to materialise, on occasions, the spirits of those who have passed over. Ian used to relate that once when on leave in England with his wife, as they were walking in a wood - the spirit of her dead husband came back to haunt them. After Ian's wife died he used to see her sometime - never direct but out on the edge of his vision. Now and again she would write to him. He would hold his pen on the paper and write, in her handwriting, and under her control. One evening Ian came to dinner with us and in the middle of dinner suddenly said "Dae (his late wife) is with us tonight, she is standing behind your chair Sis". It was quite eerie to think that her spirit was with us. He told us that as the time passed she got more distant. Many years later, after the war, we met him a couple of times in Melbourne where he had a job with the Commonwealth Department of Shipping. He was living in Geelong and had married his late wife's younger sister. On one occasion when we were passing through Melbourne we asked him to lunch with us. It so happened that we were on our way to a Moral Rearmament conference overseas. A movement in which Sis and I had become involved, a very spiritual and God centred movement. Anyway over lunch we told Ian about MRA and where we were going. He literally blew up. He started a tirade against Frank Buchman (the initiator of MRA) who was alive at that time. He then turned on us and his face became quite evil - eyes full of hatred as he tried to persuade us to cancel the trip and have nothing more to do with MRA. We parted after lunch and that was the last we ever saw of Ian MacRobert. I can only imagine that there was some evil spirit in him that was challenged by the thought of MRA. It was all quite disturbing and we talked about it many times in the following years. I will not go into the effect of MRA on our lives now it is not part of this story. However MRA did have a great and uniting effect on us and united us after a long wartime separation.

There was quite a large European community in Chefoo besides the Customs: the Hong Kong and Shanghai and the Chartered Bank of India, British and American Consuls, and a number of European business houses engaged in the import and export trade. Then there was the famous Chefoo School run by the China Inland Mission. Primarily for the children of missionaries, many other children were sent there to enjoy the good education and beautiful climate. Glorious in summer - snow and ice in winter. The Chefoo School was really quite unique. It was founded in 1881 as the "Protestant Collegiate School of CIM, Port of Chefoo, China." When the Japanese took over China, after Pearl Harbour, they closed the school at Chefoo and transferred the staff and students to Weishien, a town in central Shantung province. The Weishien Internment Camp was pretty packed. Some 1400 foreign nationals were packed into what had been the American Presbyterian Mission Compound. Now was added some 300 more from Chefoo School. The school never returned to Chefoo but the name lives on and now there are "Chefoo Schools" in Japan and Malaysia.

Of course there was the Chefoo Club, a quite magnificent club house with tennis courts, gardens and large public rooms. An essential for a European community any where in China or anywhere in the Far East for that matter. The reason for much of the European development of Chefoo was the part it played as the summer base for the American Navy which came every year from the steamy Philippines to the cool summer of North China. In summer the Chefoo club was full of Naval officers. Dinners, dances, cocktail parties in the gardens. All the residents entertained too so there was never a dull moment. Sis used to play Mah-Jong and four ladies took it in turns to have the afternoon session in their respective houses.

In summer Chefoo was a gay place. The harbour would be full of American warships and the nightclubs, bars, and brothels, full of American sailors. The girls required to man these facilities came, usually, north from Shanghai.

In winter all our visitors went away. This left the European community to its own devices.

The club reduced to what was required to cater for the locals. The night-clubs, bars and brothels shut up shop. The girls returned to Shanghai or wherever they had come from. Winter set in and it was a cold winter too. Bright warm sun but cold northerly winds. and everything under a glorious white blanket of snow. The creek, which we called "rose creek" because of its smell, had to be crossed on our way into town. It was really just an open sewer and was frozen over solidly in winter. No smell until next summer. We had two winters in Chefoo one mild, the other cold. During the cold winter the sea froze for a long way out and the harbour was frozen solid with my ship in the middle. One day I walked out to the ship. It was a bit rough and rather a struggle and of course I had to walk back again. The hard tennis courts were flooded and when built up, to about four inches of ice made a fine skating rink.

My ship, the *Huahsing,* was one of the larger of the patrol ships built under the expansion scheme, and was a sister ship to the *Feihsing* I served on some years earlier. My quarters were spacious and comfortable situated under the bridge. There were three Chinese Officers and an Italian Chief Engineer by the name of Arturo Palamadesi. She was a happy ship. We all got on well together. The second officer was Wan Tong Chu, his wife was Australian Chinese and came from Geraldton, Western Australia. Mrs Wan's Chinese was not very good and one day my steward said "Why Second Officer missie no speak Chinese"? I tried to explain that she came from Australia. I think this was too difficult as Australia meant nothing to him.

We enjoyed ourselves in Chefoo, the community was small enough for temporary residents like ourselves to become part of it. There were some interesting people and one in particular who was one of Sis' mah jong four was old Mrs Silverthorne. Part Japanese, she was quite rich and lived in a house by the harbour. Her husband had been a sea captain who settled into business in Chefoo and died there. After the Japanese occupation Mrs Silverthorne used to befriend young Japanese soldiers, who I would imagine were conscripted and out in China much against their will. The Railton family, quite large, were engaged in the export-import business. The doyen of this family, Mrs Railton, who was called "Muggy" and was another of the Mah Jong four. Another couple, with whom we were friendly, of our age were "Ginger" and Eileen Hyde. "Ginger" was in the Hong Kong and Shanghai Bank. Only a few years later, in the Stanley Internment Camp in Hong Kong, Sis saw "Ginger" and some others being taken away in a truck for execution. Eileen later died in camp and their little boy was taken care of by the wife of the manager of the Bank in Hong Kong, Lady Grayburn. Another friend, who was unmarried, was Tom Clark of the Chartered Bank of India. Years later, when my destroyer was rescuing people who had reached Padang in West Sumatra from Singapore after the surrender, we met again. We were on our way out to sea with about six hundred passengers when this dark haired man came up to me, I was wearing a beard, and said "Is your name Briggs? I said "yes" and he replied " I thought so, I'm Tom Clark, I saw a photograph of Sis in your cabin". We met again in India where I stayed with him in New Delhi when I had a spot of leave.

We had to move again after a few months, because the owners of our house were returning from overseas. Sis went house hunting and saw what she thought was just the thing. A fine stone house on the top of the Bluff overlooking the harbour, what could be better she could see my ship come and go. The house was called Otters Castle after the man who built it and because it had a row of square battlements all round the edge of the roof. The house was nice inside and Sis decided it would just do for us. Before she had decided about this because I was at sea, she met Ian MacRobert and told him about it. He was quite horrified and told her that when he first came to Chefoo he went to call on the lady who lived in the house. The servant took his card and went

Shanghai Bund. Customs House with clock. Courtesy of 'The Bulletin.'

left to right: 2nd Off. Wong, 1st Off. Wilson, Author (Captain),
Bambro (Captain of another ship). Far right Wan Tong Chu 3rd Off.

upstairs to the lady, came down and said "Missie will be down soon please wait". So Ian waited and waited, the lady was ages. Soon Ian got an awful sense of foreboding and fear and when he could stand it no longer got up and left. Please don't take that house he said it is one of the most evil houses I have ever been in. We heard afterwards that there had been some tragedy there, the house was very close to the cliff and some one had fallen over and been killed there. This was quite enough for Sis and she eventually found a fine two storey house to the East of the town.

Set on the side of the hill; there was a view of the sea, and a nice big garden. The house had a rickshaw and a gardener. When required the gardener pulled the rickshaw. I was away at sea a lot and happy to know that Alice had her own transport with a man we trusted. As a gardener he was very good and managed to keep us in some vegetables in winter grown in the bottom of a pit where the earth was still warm but had snow on top. Our Amah, Ah Koi, who came everywhere with us, a cook-boy and washerman completed the household. The men of North China do much more of this kind of work than the women; in the South washing was always a woman's job. Not forgetting the two dogs - Old Nigger, the pointer we had had for some years and Dinah, a Scotty, acquired in Chefoo. They were a great pair and gave us much enjoyment. Having to run after a big dog gradually gave the Scotty quite a good turn of speed. When getting tired she used to grab his collar. When fed up with this Old Nigger used to take her into the sea where she had to let him go before she drowned. Sis had been born in Peking (Beijing) and they say you will always go back again if you were born there, so it was arranged that she and the wife of the American Consul would make the trip. By sea to Tientsin (Tianjin) and then to Peking by rail. All was arranged but a couple of days before they left the Japanese created the Marco Polo bridge incident and marched over the border from Manchuria into North China. The Japanese had taken Manchuria from the Chinese some years before and set up a puppet state they called Manchuckuo. They installed Pu Yi, the last Emperor of China at the time of the 1911 revolution, as Emperor of Manchukuo. He had been a little boy in 1911. This is well depicted in a film called "The Last Emperor".

The main aim of Japan was to conquer China as part of a plan to expand over the whole of Asia and liberate it from the colonial Powers, in what they were pleased to call the S.E. Asia Co-Prosperity Sphere. None of this pleased the great powers, they had great and valuable interests in S.E. Asia and did not care to see them trampled on by the Japanese, now a very powerful nation.

America and Europe started to bring pressure on Japan in 1939-40 to withdraw from China and an embargo on oil, iron ore and other materials was put in place. It was this embargo which eventually caused Japan to attack Pearl Harbour in December 1941.

We did not foresee the future in 1937, but that was when the war started for us which was to go on until August 1945. However it was not until 1939 that we became involved in the war, even though up to then it had been all around us.

I had more or less a free hand as to where I went with the *Huahsing* on patrol. One of my favourite trips was to the East to call in at Weihaiwei, an island, about 3-4 miles long, guarding a lovely deep water bay with entrance from either end of the Island.

The town of Wei Hai Wei was on the mainland This was where the Royal Navy from Hong Kong used to spend the hot summer months. The entertainment was very different from the U.S. Navy's at Chefoo. The British had leased the island only and had built quite a few buildings. There was an Officers Club,a Petty Officers Club and a canteen; Club Rooms for the sailors, playing fields, tennis courts, storehouses and a few shops, completed the isalnd's facilities. One of the best known shops was Jelly Belly Tailor. He came from Hong Kong every year to answer the clothing needs of the fleet. A large sign in English and Chinese announced a name that was known to any one who had been in the Navy on the China Station.

In charge of the Chinese Customs was a Deputy Commissioner, Harold King and his wife Yvonne. She was the daughter of a French Commissioner of Customs, and had spent her life in China. Harold had a motor boat with a powerful outboard motor and I had my first experience of being towed on a board behind a fast boat. They lived in a lovely house on the mainland overlooking the sea. Once when my ship was in Chefoo, Sis and I hired a car and went to stay a couple of nights with them. It was only 30 or so miles by road from Chefoo. The Kings were keen "pontoon" or "21" players and we usually had a session.

One time when I was at Wei Hai Wei on my own and after dinner at the Kings we played pontoon, another man of the Customs staff was there too. We had an enjoyable evening and I don't remember losing any money. On this visit to Wei Hai Wei I had bought as a present for Sis, a very nice cotton lace double bed bedspread. Wei Hai Wei was famous for this particular type of coarse lace work. It was a few days before I got back to Chefoo and when I did I proudly presented my gift. Instead of smiles and thanks I was shown an angry face with the words "What did you use for money?" It took some time to find out what was wrong. It appeared the other guest at the King's "pontoon" evening had returned to Chefoo, met Sis and said, "I was playing pontoon at the Kings, Christopher was there and he lost $100!!" No wonder she was upset. $100 in those days was a lot of money. All was well in the end.

My word! it was cold at sea in the winter. I had had made, in Chefoo, a long black leather coat with a warm lining and also long leather sea boots. By adding a fur hat with ear flaps and fur gloves I was able to keep warm on the bridge and found that I never needed to wear the "long Johns" I had bought in Shanghai before we sailed North. The *Huahsing* had had her bow strengthened to enable her to push through ice. This was very necessary because when it was really cold the Western end of the Gulf was usually covered with ice that we could push through if needed. Winter at sea in these Northern waters was not very pleasant, and the storms which blew up suddenly were quite frightening.

Ashore it was different. Every winter the double windows were put in on the Northern side of the house that faced the sea. A big pot belly stove stood in the hallway and its stove pipe was connected to the pipe out through the roof. When lit this stove warmed the whole house, particularly the upstairs. Of course the days were sunny and if there was not too much wind it was a pleasure to be out. Upstairs we had a small veranda outside one of the bedrooms. This faced South, and was sheltered from the wind and collected the sun. We often used to sit out there and watch the varied traffic on the road which ran from Chefoo along the coast to the East. It was not far to the road, up the hill above our house. There were bicycles and more bicycles, hand carts, ox-drawn carts, all loaded with this and that, but very few motor cars then, just the occasional truck honking its way through the traffic. You could hear the road and its clatter far into the night.

It was 1937 and as soon as the Japanese moved into North China from Manchuria, Chinese troops began moving into Chefoo. Presumably with the idea of protecting Chefoo from invasion. They built fortifications, dug trenches on the hills behind our house, and along the sea front built a number of concrete pillboxes. All was quiet for a while and then the occasional Japanese reconnaissance planes began to appear. Slow, single engine biplanes. On the wings the flaming red ball, which some years later I grew to hate. These visitors were welcomed with small arms fire which had little or no effect. About this time British owners of property started painting

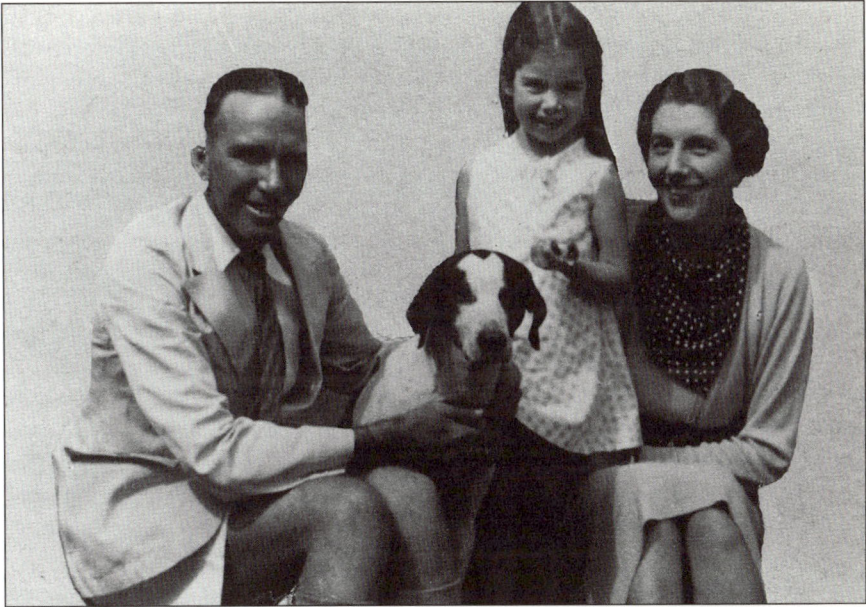

Author with Sis, Patricia and Nigger. Shanghai 1936.

'Sherwood,' our nice house in Chefoo.

Union Jacks on their roofs and flying flags to denote British property. We had a flagstaff and we hoisted the British flag too. It was felt the Japanese would not want to interfere with foreign property or harass foreigners. Within certain limits this was true and the sequestration of property and the internment of foreigners had to wait until 1941.

One day towards the end of 1937 we noticed that the Chinese soldiers had disappeared and there was not a soldier in sight. My ship was in port and we had already restricted our movements as Japanese warships were in the area. Next morning the harbour was filled with Japanese warships landing marines to take over Chefoo. It was a tense time. We were onlookers on the war between Japan and China and, as we were employed by China, we naturally worried about our position.

The Commissioner of Customs was informed that my ship was not to go to sea without permission and that a sentry would be placed on board. When I next went out to the ship there was a Japanese marine with a huge rifle on duty. I suppose the rifle was the ordinary size but it looked huge when held by such a small man. We duly saluted each other and that was that as he had no English. Next day when I went to the ship they said the sentry had not been fed and had asked the crew for rice. By this time most of the warships had gone but a guardship was moored at the outer breakwater near the harbour entrance. She was a big merchant ship converted for Naval use with a big crew of officers, sailors, and marines. I sent one of the officers over in our boat to ask them for food for the sentry which duly arrived. The next thing was that sentry wanted to use one of our spare cabins to sleep at night. This seemed rather odd to me so I took our boat and went to call on the guardship. A senior officer took charge of me and I put the question about a cabin for the sentry. The answer struck me as quite Asian. "Yes, he can have a cabin to use at night but during the day he must be up on deck where he can be seen". Eventually, after a week or so of this, the sentry was taken away and not replaced.

One of the *Huahsing's* regular jobs was visiting the small Customs Stations along the coast which controlled the junk trade and also the intermediate visits to a couple of lighthouses. The big lighthouse tender from Shanghai only called twice a year but we visited monthly.

Our first trip to sea, after the Japanese invasion, was to visit a Customs Station. We had permission, but the Commissioner was told a Japanese Officer would come with me. A young sub-lieutenant with a little English came on board and we duly sailed. I said he was to stay on the bridge with me. Soon we were out in the open sea and there was a strong wind. It was quite rough with a short steep sea and *Huahsing* could roll violently. It was not long before the poor Japanese officer was a casualty and as I refused to let him go below he had to stay on the bridge with a bucket. My sailors passed rude remarks about him in Chinese, some of which he may have understood. It was only a day trip and we returned to port that night but it was the last time they sent an officer with me. Too much loss of face for the Japanese Navy.

We were, naturally I suppose, very anti-Japanese. They had started a war against a China that employed us and treated us well. They had invaded the place which was our home. Their attitude was threatening. A feeling of insecurity and fear had interrupted our peaceful and relaxed attitude to life and our prospects for the future were beginning to look uncertain. We were prepared to do anything which would embarrass the unwanted invaders, without getting ourselves or even the Customs into trouble.

Huahsing was sent to sea to visit the lighthouse keeper and his staff of Howki Island light, about 40 miles to the West. We carried their mail, fresh food and anything that they had asked for. I went ashore to have a chat with the lightkeeper, a European. One of his grumbles was that he had a visit from a Japanese destroyer. An officer and some sailors had come ashore and searched the lightstation. The officer confiscated the lightkeeper's privately owned short wave radio. His one means of knowing what was going on in the wide world, especially in China.

The Japanese officer made one mistake, he signed the visitors book in English giving his name, his rank and the name of the ship. It was now over to me. We returned to Chefoo and I put in a report to the Commissioner. Dick Foster-Hall promptly sent the story off to the Inspector General in Shanghai.

I thought that this would be the end of the matter, but a month or six weeks later a message came for me to go on board the Japanese guard ship. Off I went, in my best uniform, in our spick and span motor boat; boat's crew in best uniform; bowman at attention with his boat book in the correct Naval fashion. I marched up the gangway, saluted smartly and was taken off to see the Commander, not the ship's Captain but the executive officer. I was asked to sit down and was informed that Lieutenant X, the officer who confiscated the radio was in very much trouble. I was asked to convey his apologies to the lightkeeper and to return to him all that was left of the radio, a cardboard box containing an assortment of radio parts. This I did on our next trip to the lighthouse and we had a good laugh about it. Then the Commander asked if I would have lunch with them in the wardroom, to which I replied that I would be delighted. Inwardly I was looking forward to a lovely Japanese lunch. We proceeded to the wardroom where I was introduced to the other officers - there must have been 30 or more in a large wardroom. I was given a whiskey and then another and time went on and no lunch - more whiskey and still no lunch. Then we were called to sit down and what should it be but a European lunch of very tough grilled steak, vegetables and a boiled pudding of some sort. Bitter disappointment for me. I said my farewells and went ashore feeling a bit disgruntled about the lunch. However, as soon as I thought it over rationally, I realized what a warm compliment I had been paid. That all those officers should have had to wait over an hour for a lunch, which I am sure they did not like, just for me. It was indeed a compliment and an honour.

The Japanese Navy were always fairly easy to deal with and did not seem to be imbued with the arrogance of the Japanese army. The Navy was modelled on the British Royal Navy and, presumably, this says it all During the war, yet to come, men who were rescued from their sunken ships were usually well treated and it was not until they were put ashore and handed over to the army that their hard time commenced.

About this time Dick Foster-Hall, our well liked Commissioner of Customs, was replaced by a Japanese. There were a number of Japanese in the Chinese Customs in various positions.

One very senior man was a Mr Ishii. He could have been Deputy Inspector General or Chief Secretary. The Japanese man now appointed as Commissioner to Chefoo was elderly and had just retired. He arrived in Japan to be greeted with a letter instructing him to return to China and take over Chefoo. He was a very charming man and I had to take him to visit Weihaiwei and our other Customs Stations by sea. Sitting in my cabin after lunch one day he said "You know Briggs this is the worst thing my country has ever done" (attempting to conquer China) "I do not know how it will end." In fact it ended in tragedy for Japan.

The Japanese army were everywhere and they were a nuisance because one was never quite sure what they might do. One constantly felt the need to be careful of them, A few instances come to mind. The ship had been to sea this day and I was coming home on my bicycle along the road by the sea front. In the distance I spotted a Japanese sentry with his back to me and his rifle with a fixed bayonet across his shoulder. I was going quite slowly when he heard me and he swung round and caught me across the chest with his rifle. It was quite dark by now and he put his hand up to my face, and felt the beard which I then had. Realising that with a beard like that I must be a foreigner, he let me go on. Another time on the same road in daylight I saw two Japanese soldiers. One had a bandage round his head, stained red, and was holding his rifle with the bayonet fixed. He was standing on top of one of the Chinese concrete pillboxes and the other soldier was taking his photograph. I waved as I went past and they smiled back.

Sis in her rickshaw, all wrapped up against the cold, was going home one afternoon after being out playing mah-jong. Along came a Japanese lorry full of armed soldiers and stopped our rickshaw. Our rickshaw man was terrified - Sis wondered what was going to happen with all these rifles pointed at her. An officer got out of the cab, took her photograph, got back into the cab and drove off. You never knew quite what might happen, though they did leave us alone on that occasion. At that time I do not think Japan wanted to involve foreign powers.

Christmas 1937 was now over and I had some very good news. A letter from the Inspector General informed me that my contract was cancelled, I had originally been employed on a six year contract, and I was to become a member of the permanent staff. In addition I was informed that we were to go on twelve months leave as from 15th April 1938. The usual conditions of employment with the CMC was 12 months leave after the first six years, and then after every five years.

This was all good news indeed. My health had deteriorated over the last months, and a lot of it I put down to the continual strain of living under the Japanese and in constant fear. Nowadays you would call it 'stress related'. This meant my future was assured, and I was in a job and a country that I had grown to love, or so I thought. We had had a glorious 18 months in Chefoo in spite of the Japanese. Packing up again; we were used to it, and finding homes for Nigger and Dinah the sad part - we both get very fond of our animals. Our passages were booked on a P. & O. ship that we were to pick up in Hong Kong. The family again took ship, complete with the faithful Ah Koi, and on the way to Hong Kong we picked up some well to do and many poorer Chinese passengers. They were fleeing from the Japanese, who by this time were more or less in control of Shanghai and were fighting their way inland and towards the South.

One of the well to do families offered Ah Koi a job. When we asked why she did not take it she said "Chinese family too much play mah jong, drink tea all night, I have to stay up". She was waiting for us when we got back in 1939 having spent the year in her home village.

The Japanese gave the Chinese a very hard time indeed, millions must have lost their lives between 1937 and 1945. Unbelievable cruelty was rained on the Chinese population and they were executed by the sword at the slightest excuse.

Some months before, Ah Koi's son had been in Shanghai and she had asked for leave to go and see him. We gave her a month's leave with pay, well deserved, and got a very nice elderly Chinese lady with bound feet as a temporary amah. The month went by and no Ah Koi and no word from her. We began to get worried as there was heavy fighting in and around Shanghai, though not in the International Settlement as far as we knew. Eventually after another two or three weeks she turned up with a tale of heavy fighting and bombing and the difficulty of getting back to Chefoo. My word!. We were glad to see her and gave her a most affectionate welcome; we had got very fond of our Ah Koi and had been very concerned for her safety.

Chapter 10

A YEAR AT HOME
1938 - 1939

The P. & O. ship we boarded in Hong Kong, took us a month to get home. It was a great joy to arrive in England towards the end of May 1938. I had been away from home for just over six years, and Sis nearly five. Never before had I ever had a year's leave on full pay. A whole year to do what we liked, go where we liked, spend time with our parents and on what was quite good pay in those days, £36 a month or £9 a week, $72 and $18 respectively. Times were not too good in England and £9 a week was about twice the average wage.

Sis's parents were living in London, in a private hotel. My father-in-law was still working though he retired soon after we went back to China. The first thing to get was transport and we bought a new Ford Prefect, dark blue, from the Ford Company's showroom in Upper Regent Street, it cost £142-10-0.

After going to see my parents in Wales we decided to find a place we could use as a permanent home. Sis looked through the advertisements in "The Lady" and saw one for a cottage at Nettlebed in Oxfordshire. Off we went in our new car to see it and found it was called "The Birds Nest" and was owned by a Mrs Finch. It was not, however, a lovely warm old cottage with a thatched roof as we had hoped but a rather "jerry" built two story weekender. Built of timber and some sort of prefab wall slabs, the drafts came through everywhere. It was quite pretty, in a quiet lane off the main road.

We had forgotten how lovely England can be in early June, everything green, flowers, wildflowers and the trees. Nettlebed was well situated for us. It was on the main road to Wales and also handy to London. Our shopping town was Henley-on-Thames, a beautiful place in its own right.

Come July, Sis and I decided that we would go off on our own, and, via a visit to my parents, go on to Scotland. My mother-in-law and Sis's Aunt Lina were available to look after Patricia. We borrowed a bivouac tent, added a primus stove, simple cooking and eating utensils, bedding and warm clothes, and off we went.

We stayed with my parents in Aberayron for a few days. It gave my mother, whose eyesight was now rather poor great joy to be taken out in the car. We took her to Aberystwyth to shop and to see my Uncle Godfrey - father's brother who now lived near Aberystwyth. Even my father condescended to come with me, though I do not remember the four of us ever going anywhere.

Fashions were changing in 1938, women were wearing slacks, and Sis found they were very comfortable for motoring. The car had no heating and England is seldom warm even in summer.

My father was very anxious that if we went up the West Coast, we went to see his Aunt Emmy, my only great Aunt alive at that time. She was reputed to be rich, was in her 90's and lived in a lovely old black and white house in the village of Scorton in Lancashire. It was about half way between Lancaster and Preston just off the main road. We were warned to be on our best behaviour and told that she probably had a butler and a staff of servants. The day to set off arrived and Sis donned her slacks to travel in and went to my fathers room to say good bye. He took one look at her and said "Don't go and see Aunt Emmy in those comic opera pants!" He was assured that she would change on arrival and off we went. She had been warned we were coming to see her and we were expected to stay the night.

It was a long way from Aberayron to Scorton and some of it was slow through Wigan and the "black country" so it was late, probably about 6 pm when we arrived at the lovely house at the end of a shady driveway. We were met at the front door not by a butler, but by a woman who was companion, housekeeper, and nurse to old Aunt Emmy. We were welcomed and Sis asked if she could go straight to our room and change. The reply was that we were expected to go straight up to see Aunt Emmy. She was in bed and would settle down for the night as soon as she had seen us and had her evening meal. So upstairs we went to meet a smiling and friendly old lady propped up in bed. We introduced ourselves and the first thing Aunt Emmy said, looking at Sis, was "What a good idea to wear trousers when travelling". She then turned to me and said "I hope you are a nicer man than your father". I don't know what lay behind that remark but I often felt that he was not very popular with his family. We had a long and relaxed talk with the old lady, telling her all about my job in China and about my parents. We were then shown to our room, and soon dinner and bed. We had had a long day and were not then used to driving long distances. Next morning we said goodbye to Aunt Emmy and took to the road again.

This was not the first time I had been to Scorton. When we were living in Ireland and I was between eleven and twelve I was invited to go and stay with my father's cousin Peter Ormrod and his family who owned Wyresdale Park at Scorton. Wyresdale was a huge estate with a very large house, farm and farm houses. It was on the river Wyre and the land extended up into uncultivated moors. Cousin Peter had a farm school on the place where the students paid to come and learn farming and Peter got the benefit of the cheap labour. There was a daughter of the house who would have been about 16 possibly 17 and as it was holiday time she was at home. She had a pony and one was provided for me and she spent a lot of time showing me around and riding on the moors. They even had a trout hatchery on the river, some of these went into the Wyre for the owner's fishing. The surplus was sold. I fell in love with this cousin, the first girl of that age that I had ever known. I kept her photo for some years. If it had not been for her my visit would not have been much fun as nobody else, adults, seemed interested in entertaining me.

I don't remember much about cousin Peter except that he was a large and rather florid man who was friendly and kind to me. There were lots of servants and dinner was definitely formal. Everybody dressed for dinner and met in the drawing room until dinner was ready. I used to wear my Eton suit, worn on Sunday at school, for dinner. An Eton suit consisted of dark grey or black trousers, short black "bumfreezer" jacket. A very deep starched white collar was worn and the collar came out over the jacket collar and a black tie. The first night at dinner my wineglass was filled like everyone else's and when it was time to stand up I was definitely "woozy". I learned to be careful in future. It was of course a "sporting" estate. Grouse shooting on the moors, pheasants in the woodlands and fishing in the river. Lancashire is a lovely county and varies from the desolate black industrial part to glorious country and moorland.

The Ormrods were rich industrial people. The money had been made out of cotton spinning over the years and they had acquired large estates and built large houses. My paternal grandmother had been an Ormrod, a good Lanchashire name. The last time we were in Britain I inquired about Wyresdale and I understand it is now some sort of institution and the moorland has been returned to the public.

We continued our journey and crossed the border into Scotland at Gretna Green. We then started looking for somewhere to camp and soon spotted a place by a stream not far from the road. We pitched our little tent, lit the Primus stove and made ourselves baked beans on toast. We had no modern sleeping bags or air mattresses only blankets, a groundsheet and it was very hard and later very cold. I think there was a frost we were so high up. Another night we camped above Fort William, up in the hills where there was thick bracken. We stamped out a flat bit and pitched the tent. That night it was more comfortable on the bracken. We did not use the tent again on the trip.

The rest of our tour was without incident and the only real highlight was a visit to the 1938 Empire Exhibition at Glasgow. We arrived near the exhibition ground just as it was getting dark. The answer "ask a policeman". We did and he told us of a bed and breakfast house quite close. It was a beautifully clean house run by a lovely lady who gave us a most magnificent and sustaining Scottish breakfast. We saw the exhibition and went on our way. We got as far as John O'Groats and came back down the East Coast stopping at Edinburgh and back to Nettlebed via my parents in Aberayron.

Patricia went for two terms to her first school in Wallingford, a pretty little town, on the Thames. It was a boarding school, run by the Misses Hedges, and I am afraid she hated it but she needed to go to school, she was nearly six. It left us free to visit relatives.

At Christmas it snowed. Nettlebed was fairly high and it was very cold. All the family, at least Sis's family came over Christmas. We even got my mother from Wales for a few days and then took her back to Aberayron.

During this time in Britain there had been the fear that war was going to break out. Trenches were being dug, important buildings were being sandbagged, in fact a real general panic. Mr Chamberlain, the Prime Minister, was negotiating with Hitler and he arrived back waving that famous piece of paper and saying there would be peace in our time. Everybody heaved a sigh of relief and got on with their work but the feeling of fear and uncertainty remained. Our time was drawing to a close and we were due to report in Shanghai on or before 15 April 1939.

We decided to return to China via America and the Pacific. The Customs' agents booked us on the *Queen Mary* to New York, then to Montreal by train, and across Canada to Vancouver and then the Canadian Pacific Steamships' *Empress of Russia*. Our farewells were sadly said as it was back to China for 5 years. Even though Chamberlain had said peace in our time, there was a sense of foreboding and we did not go back with a great feeling of security for the future. When we left the house in Aberayron, with my parents waving from the little white gate in the high hedge, I turned to Sis and said, "I wonder if we will ever see them again". We only saw my father again as my mother died in 1943.

We joined the *Queen Mary* in Southampton and to our joy found we had been given a lovely 1st class cabin instead of the 2nd class to which we were entitled to. Three beds, large wardrobe, arm chairs and its own facilities, real luxury. The four days across the Atlantic were particularly calm and as far as I remember Sis stood up to it well. We had a night in New York and then to Montreal to join the Canadian Pacific Railway for the trip to Vancouver. Steam train of course, and though they kept the train as clean as possible everything was soon covered in black dust. We stopped at Winnipeg one morning early and went for a short walk. It was bitterly cold and soon Patricia was in tears because her knees were so cold, so we returned to the warm train. Through Calgary - I wondered where my father's ranch had been. Through the Rockies - snow still on the ground, pine forest clinging to the mountainside - some of the world's most spectacular scenery and then Vancouver. We had two days in Vancouver at a nice hotel. We put Patricia in a bath as soon as we got to the hotel and the water got so dirty with her first wash we ran it out and refilled it. Crawling on the floor and seats of the railway carriage had left its mark. We visited the relatives of some friends in the U.K. and explored lovely Vancouver and then off to Shanghai in the *Empress of Russia*

Some years ago there was a song in one of the Fred Astaire films which said "The Pacific isn't terrific and the Atlantic isn't gigantic". The Pacific may not be terrific but it certainly is not pacific. The North Pacific is one of the world's roughest oceans and the great circle course taken by our ship went in a great curve to the North from Vancouver and it was very rough. Poor Sis was really sea sick this time, even though she had taken seasick tablets. The trip from Vancouver to Yokohama took 12 days and Sis was in bed for every one of them. At last the calm of the Inland Sea of Japan. Sis got up, went to the bathroom and fainted. She was very weak, but quickly recovered and the rest of the trip was in fine weather.

At Shanghai we were told that we had been appointed to the Kowloon Customs which is what the Hong Kong set up, explained previously, is called and I was appointed in Command of *C.P.S. Haiping*. So we continued on to Hong Kong in our Empress.

By this time the Japanese, in their attempt to conquer China had worked their way down through the costal provinces until they had surrounded Hong Kong. Their warships patrolled the coast and our Customs ships were not allowed to go to sea and were peacefully anchored in Kowloon Bay. A somewhat lazy life ensued and I used to go off to the ship in the morning and deal with any business and then home to lunch, tennis at the USRC (United Services Recreation Club), golf at Fanling, or just a walk in the hills.

We had taken a big house in Kowloon from some people named Odell who had gone to Europe. A very nice house, high up, with quite a view. Unfortunately the owner was a cigar smoker, and the house reeked of cigar smoke and though we got a bit used to it, the smell was still there when we left some months later.

The time went swiftly, renewing acquaintance with old friends. It was important that Patricia continued with the education she had started in England. Good education was available in Hong Kong so we enrolled her in a local school. Our dear Ah Koi was waiting for us. She had spent the last year in her village but had found out all about us and when we were due back. We kept on the cook, coolie, and gardener that were employees of the Odell's, so Ah Koi had an easy time doing the washing and acting as ladies maid.

On the 2nd of September Sis became ill, and next morning the doctor said she had developed dysentery and I took her to Kowloon Hospital. By this time the situation in Europe was very tense and Britain had just issued an ultimatum to Germany over her invasion of Poland. Late that afternoon we were listening to the radio by Sis's bed and the announcement that we were at war with Germany came through. To say we were devastated would be an understatement. All the future we had looked forward to crashed at that moment. What it would bring we did not know but we were quite sure it would never be the same again and there was the additional worry of our families in Britain. Japan was threatening but so far was not involved - though they were all around Hong Kong.

Sis was not in hospital more than a few days and fortunately she had not been nearly as ill as she was the first time she had dysentery. We were always very careful about our food but when you have servants and are not doing it yourself, you can never be quite sure what goes on in your kitchen.

Once things had settled down and Sis was better I said one morning that I thought I should join the Navy. This was agreed to and off I went to *HMS Tamar* to offer my services. *Tamar* was an old warship tied up in the basin in the Naval dockyard. She was used as the administrative headquarters of the Navy and contained the Commodore's office and all the various naval staff. I was interviewed but was told there was nothing for me and they would let me know in due course. So that was that. I went on looking after my ship and soon we had to move house.

The Odell's had come back early so we moved out into a lovely modern first floor flat in Eu Gardens almost opposite the Kowloon hospital. Three bedrooms, three bathrooms,. nice lounge, kitchen and servants quarters. It was expensive but I was getting Commanders rent allowance which covered it. So we waited and by the end of September no word from the Navy. A couple of our men who had also volunteered and got no answer went to see the Canadian Trade Commissioner to ask if Canada wanted volunteers for their Navy. The answer came quickly and Canada paid their families passages. However for better or worse I stuck to the Royal Navy. One day in October I went to my ship and there was no Chief Engineer. My Chief was Arturo Palamedesi. He and his wife were great friends of ours and we used to visit each others home. He had been my Chief Engineer of the *Huahsing* in Chefoo so our acquaintance was of long standing. About noon that day we had our answer. Italy had joined the war in Europe on the side of Germany. The Palamedesi family, probably as the result of a tip-off from the Italian Consul had slipped over to Macau. Thereby evading the chance of being interned by the British in Hong Kong.

Towards the end of October I was asked to attend for a medical examination on HMS Tamar. This was successful and I was asked when I could join. The 1st of November was decided on and I put in my resignation to the Chinese Maritime Customs. On the 1st November 1939 I ceased to be a Commander in the CMC and became a Lieutenant in the Royal Naval Reserve. My Naval career commenced with my appointment to one of the local destroyers, for training. Some weeks went by and I was moved to *HMS Scout* as 1st Lieutenant (Executive Officer). In mid-1940, all Service wives were evacuated to Australia, for reasons which to this day are still unclear. After some months, I succeeded in getting permission for her to return to Hong Kong. On the way she left Patricia in the care of cousins in Manila. He was the manager of the Shell Company there, fearing she would not be allowed to land if accompanied by a child. Owing to the shortage of skilled European women in Hong Kong, after the evacuation, Sis quickly got a job as a secretary with Dodwells, one of the larger Hong Kong companies. That was the situation up to December 1941.

The day the Japanese entered the war, *HMS Scout* sailed, in company with one of the other local defence destroyers, for Singapore via Manila. Hong Kong surrendered on Christmas day, a very sad day for me, and Sis was interned in Stanley Civilian Internment Camp. Patricia and my cousins were interned when the Philipines surrendered early in 1942.

I stood on the Liverpool landing stage, one cold and miserable day in early November 1945, to watch the *SS Empress of Australia* arrive, bringing with her ex-prisoners of war and civilian internees from the Far East. My Lovely Lady was on board, a shadow of her former self, but alive and in moderate health. Patricia had arrived home some months earlier via the USA.

The full story of Sis's war experiences will be found in her book; From Peking to Perth by Alice Briggs, published in 1984 by Artlook Books, Perth, Western Australia.

H.M.S. Scout

Author as Lieutenant, Royal Naval Reserve.

Chapter 11

WHAT HAPPENED TO THE CHINESE MARITIME CUSTOMS? 1945 - 1949

I left the Service in 1939 and it continued under Japanese duress, with the Inspectorate still in Shanghai, until December 1941 when the World War spread to the Far East. The Inspector General and all the staff of Allied nationality in occupied areas were removed from office and interned. Maze himself was repatriated in 1942 and retired from the Service in 1943, after reporting to the Government in Chungking. He was awarded the KCMG and the KBE.

An Inspectorate was set up in Chungking under Mr.C.H.B.Joly, a British Commissioner, who was appointed Officiating Inspector General to take control of all Customs offices and staff at places not under the Japanese. "Bingo" Joly as he was nicknamed was a great friend of ours and Sis had been to stay with him and his wife Dolly when he was Commissioner in Hainan. We returned the compliment by having Dolly to stay when she visited Hong Kong.

In the middle of 1943 both Maze and Joly retired and Mr Lester K. Little, an American, was appointed I.G.. Little had been the Commissioner in Canton when it was occupied by the Japanese who placed him under house arrest. He was later repatriated and returned to Chungking to take up his post

At the end of the war I was working in what was then the Admiralty in London. My office was in Queen Anne's Mansions and when I looked out of my window I looked down on the ruins of the Guards Chapel which had been hit by a flying bomb. This happened during a service there, and the loss of life was very heavy.

One morning in January 1946 my telephone rang and I answered it to find the London resident Commissioner of Chinese Customs on the line. "Would you like to come back to China said the voice"? "Certainly I would" was my reply. "How soon can you be ready?" "Well I need to be demobilised but it should only be a few weeks". So far so good and my heart leaped at the idea of going back to China and resuming the career that I had loved and the country. Then the blow fell. The voice said "You won't be able to take your wife. The country is very disturbed. The money is inflated to a fantastic extent and we are not allowing any wives to return." My reply was immediate. I would not go back without my wife who had only returned from her Japanese internment camp in Hong Kong in November 1945. She was not at all well and was still recovering from 3½ years of malnutrition. I was told they were sorry about my reply as they would have liked me to return. As it happened I think I did the right thing. Even if I had been able to take Sis, it all ended with the Communists in 1949. The Kuomintang Government escaped to Formosa (Taiwan) and the Customs staff were left to fend for themselves.

War ended in 1945 and when the Japanese left China, they left it in chaos. L.K. Little, the Inspector General, rapidly searched for ex-staff members willing to return to China. One of those who returned was Captain F.L. Sabel, an American, who had been a Deputy Coast

Inspector when I worked in the Custom House in 1935-36. He was already Coast Inspector and was given the task of rebuilding all the activities of the Coast Department from nothing.

Captain Sabel was an interesting character. Some people did not get on with him though I did, and he had been very helpful to a "new chum" in the office. He was down to earth and not afraid to say what he felt. He was a real sailor having first gone to sea in sailing ships. He rounded Cape Horn once in a four master and twice rounded Cape of Good Hope in a three masted full rigged ship. One of his voyages was from Bunbury to Antwerp which took 140 days. I would imagine with a load of timber though he does not say in his letters. The Great War saw him in the U.S. Navy and he was a Lieutenant in 1919. He must have joined the Customs soon after the Great War because he was in command of a Customs Cruiser in 1927. During World War II he remained employed by the Customs, had been promoted to Coast Inspector and was on "Special Duty" in the United States and in constant touch with L.K. Little also an American. Sabel returned to Shanghai as soon as the Japanese left in 1945 and the first job to be tackled was replacing the light buoys from the entrance of the Yangtze and upstream. Few of the aids were functioning when the Japanese left and Sabel was able to call upon the U.S. Navy for assistance because the Customs had no buoy tender and a lack of staff. Even the Shanghai Pilot Boat was a US Navy vessel. While in the U.S. Sabel had selected some electrically operated lights for the light-buoys and these were the first of that kind on the Yangtze and a great improvement on the old oil lanterns of former years. A set of batteries would last four months and gradually the lighting extended up and down the river.

The restoration of the lighting on the river made possible the escape of the British and American Navy ships from the Communists in their night runs down the river.

When the Japanese took over Shanghai in 1942 they had swiftly ejected Sabel from the lovely Coast Inspectors house at 75 Route Ferguson, where Sis and I used to enjoy vodka and caviar on the lawns in the comparative cool of a hot Shanghai evening with our good friends the Carrels. Sabel says in a letter "They did a good job of cleaning me out". He lost everything including valuable records and photographs.

I have no record of how Sabel got out of Shanghai. In 1942 the Japanese repatriated Americans living in China and Hong Kong, in exchange for Japanese residents living in the USA. A neutral ship, Portugese, was used for the repatriation and I presume this was how Sabel managed to spend the rest of the war years in his home country.

In 1946 the Custom Houses on Taiwan returned to Chinese control after 50 years under the Japanese. In 1948 the Government had instructed the Inspector General of Customs to transfer the gold reserves to Taiwan. Some 200 tons of gold and silver were transferred in small Customs vessels, recently purchased as surplus from the Americans, even though Chinese warships were available, again showing the trust that the Government placed in the Chinese Maritime Customs.

The foreign staff who returned to China were, in the end treated very badly by the Kuomintang Government by now in Taiwan. Negotiations about pay had been going on between the Inspector General and Dr.H.H. Kung who was the Minister of Finance. Sabel met Dr.Kung a number of times in America but being in a subordinate position could not bring up the subject as that was really for the I.G. to deal with. The I.G. however sent copies of Sabel's letters about pay and conditions direct to the Ministry of Finance. In one of the replies to the I.G., Dr.Kung wrote "Captain Sabel need not be concerned, we shall show gratitude, and take care of everybody." In another letter Dr.Kung said "China will not let down those who have been faithful and loyal to the Service." What actually happened when the Government fled to Taiwan was very different. In the next four years the rebuilding proceeded apace. The Customs service was reformed and the Coast Department got on with the job. until Shanghai was captured by the Communist forces on May 25 1949. The day before this the National Garrison Commander had ordered Sabel's arrest. The reason was that owing to the lack of officers and crew, who deserted in force, he was unable to comply with the demand to hand over all the Customs ships as he had been ordered to do, they wanted the vessels for the withdrawal of troops and equipment. Sabel found it almost a relief to be in the hands of the Communists next day. Sabel was, generally speaking, treated fairly well. Of course there were incidents at times, and no possible way to get out. The only really difficult time was when they had him up for a four day inquiry, and threatened him with a possible Military tribunal. He writes "Anyhow, it was a happy day when I was permitted to leave by a French steamer to Hong Kong". Before he was allowed to leave Shanghai Sabel, had to hand over all photographs and documents for clearance. Very little was returned.

Captain Sabel then took a job in Japan under the Occupation Authorities as Administrator Navigational Aids. He left Japan in the summer of 1952.

Shortly before the arrival of the Communists, L.K.Little, the Inspector General, was ordered by the Minister of Finance to select Customs staff (Chinese) to accompany him to Canton and then to Taiwan. Here a Customs administration was set up which has continued to function under a series of Chinese Inspectors General. Little went to Taiwan with them and retired in 1950 but remained as Adviser to the Ministry of Finance until 1954. The Customs functions in Taiwan today on the lines that have been followed for the last 100 years.

I am glad that we never went back to China. To get reorganised after the war, in the two areas of family relations and occupation were difficult enough for us as it was, without the added burden of a failed job in China and four years wasted. Instead we spent the four years in England and on 24 December 1948 we sailed for Australia and arrived in Fremantle in January 1949. A move I have never regretted. Australia has been good to us.

Owing to our move to Australia I lost touch with many of the friends that we had made during our time in China. In Perth, Western Australia there were a small number of ex-staff members of the C.M.C.. One was John Hope who I knew well, he was Australian and his wife was English. We visited them often in Perth until his death some years ago. His father had been the greatly respected Dr.Hope of Fremantle. John's wife returned to England after his death. Then there was Commander Eric Sexton, who had been a member of the river staff stationed at various ports up the Yangtze. After war broke out he managed to escape from Chungking and got to India. At this time the whole Chinese coast was in the hands of the Japanese and to get out of China you had to "go over the hump". In other words by air to India, over the Himalayas.

He joined the Royal Indian Navy and when the war finished and India had been partitioned he transferred to the Pakistan navy and finally retired with the rank of Commander. He settled in Western Australia at Albany. His great interest was the local Naval Cadets which he cared for for many years and by the time of his death had become a much respected member of the Albany community.

Then there is my old friend Captain Wan. His name is Wan Tong Chu and he was my third officer when I was in command of the *Huahsing* in Chefoo. Since returning to Australia he has spent the years in the very profitable Chinese restaurant trade and is the owner of the first

Captain T.C. Wan & Author, 1995.

class Canton Restaurant in Hay Street, Perth, now assisted by his daughter Shirley and her brother Brian. Wan had been in Australia during the war years and held a British passport as he was born in Malaya when it was British. He married an Australian lady. He was one of the old staff who returned to Shanghai after the Japanese had been ousted and was appointed Harbour Officer first class and was working in Shanghai. I presume that there was no seagoing patrol work and the job of the Coast Department would have been the re-establishment of harbours, pilotage, coastal lighting, and opening the Yangtze to navigation. All seems to have been going well until the communists began to approach Shanghai and the Nationalists began to prepare to run for it.

About this time all the Customs staff received letters from the Communist authorities telling of the imminent takeover, asking for their continued loyalty and warning against disruption. The end was near and the Nationalists were shipping to Formosa (Taiwan) soldiers, military equipment, archives, and everything else, that could be used in Formosa. They had commandeered a Chinese registered ship which was owned by a company in Hong Kong. For this ship they needed a captain. So the Customs were told to send Captain Wan Tong Chu and insisted that no one else would do. Wan took command of the ship and started the ferrying of personnel and material from the mainland to Taiwan - even from as far away as Hainan Island. It was obviously no use the Nationalists going to Taiwan unless they took as much of the wherewithal in the way of ships, men, planes, and stores. Without a means of defence the Communists could easily have gone on to take back Taiwan, which even today is still regarded as a province of China. This ship under Nationalist control was not at all what Wan saw for himself. His wife and two children were in Hong Kong and he wanted to join them as soon as possible and presumably return to Australia. This ferrying went on for some time until the whole of China was in Communist hands and there could be no more trips back to the mainland. For some reason the ship was sent to Japan and after discharge was ordered to return to Taiwan. At this point Wan saw his chance - he had no intention of working for either the Nationalists or the Communists - so he made the decision to escape with the ship to Hong Kong. Proceeding south from Japan to Taiwan was simple because he was on his expected course, but to pass down the strait between Taiwan and the mainland saw the severe risk of being spotted by Nationalist or Communist planes or warships.

The God of good fortune must have been on his side because as soon as he headed down the Formosa Strait a thick fog descended. By the time it had cleared the ship had passed the island and was well on its way to Hong Kong. Safely in Hong Kong, Wan had to bargain with the ship's owner. Finally it was arranged that he would hand over the ship on payment of three months salary in U.S. dollars. This agreed the Wan family returned to Australia where we were to meet up with them fairly soon after we arrived. Over the years the family have prospered.

The two children, Shirley and Brian, are both married and we developed a friendship which has remained constant. There is something in friends you have known for some sixty years, with whom one has so much in common.

THE END

Appendix 1

LIFE AND DEATH OF HMS CONWAY
1839 - 1953

The system of training for the greatly diminished merchant navy of today changed in the early 1970's and the idea of these training establishments was abandoned and training for the sea became a part of Technical Education with sea experience interspersed with technical training ashore. So ended some 115 years of training for sea service the Conway way.

In 1859 the Admiralty lent *HMS Conway,* a full rigged frigate of 650 tons, to the MMSA (Mercantile Marine Service Association) to be used as a training ship. She was towed to the Mersey and anchored off Rock Ferry. She was fitted to cater for the training of 120 boys. The first *Conway* performed so well that it was soon found to be too small and the committee of the MSA asked Admiralty for the loan of larger ship. This was granted and *HMS Winchester,* a fourth-rate full rigged ship of the 60-gun Taya class frigates arrived in the Mersey in November 1861. The Admiralty considered it a good idea to perpetuate the name and so the *Winchester* became the second *Conway.* This ship lasted until 1875 when the Admiralty was asked again for a larger ship. This was granted and Captain Edward Franklin, then the Captain Superintendent of the *Conway* went to Devonport to inspect the Nile. He found the Nile acceptable, but quite a lot of work needed doing before taking her to Liverpool This is where my interest comes in because *Nile* was the *Conway* in which I served my two years 1921-1923.

It is worthwhile looking at *HMS Nile* as a battleship and at her interesting career. She was laid down at Devonport in 1827 as a second rate ship of the line with 92 guns and was not launched until 12 years later. On June 28 1839she was christened *HMS NILE* by Miss Warren, the daughter of Admiral Frederick Warren, Superintendent of the Dockyard. Some 50,000 people turned out to see the launch, with the usual music from Naval and Military bands. She was 4,375 tons, by the 1834 method of measurement and a length of 240 feet, a beam of 54 feet and depth of 58 feet. This quite massive ship cost 86,197 to build and equip, she was finished off with a figurehead of Horatio, Admiral Lord Nelson.

Her designer, Sir Robert Seppings, a famous naval architect and Surveyor General of the Navy had introduced some revolutionary ideas regarding the laying of ships timbers. These ideas were much criticised but were used in the construction of *NILE,* but the fact was, she was in perfect condition after being afloat for some 115 years.

She was, however, not commissioned until 1852 some 13 years after she was launched and 25 years after she was laid down. She was not completely a sailing ship for long because after a few months she was docked at Devonport and fitted with engines and a propeller. The funnel which looked like an ugly stovepipe came up just behind the foremast. The screw could be pulled up out of the way when she was under sail alone. On her trial trip as a steamship she attained 6.85 knots.

HMS Nile became one of the ships of the fleet engaged in the Baltic against the Russians in 1854. Again in 1855 she went to the Baltic and helped to destroy some transports in the Bay of Vistanemi. In September she used her boats to board and burn some Russian vessels anchored there. Peace with Russia came in 1856 and Nile went to North America and the West Indies. She returned to Devonport in 1857 and was the flag ship at Queenstown in 1858. In the following year she came home again and had new boilers fitted at Devonport. In 1860 she sailed to become the flagship on the North America and West Indies station. In March 1864 she returned to Devonport and was paid off into reserve until in June 1875 she was allocated on loan by the Admiralty to the Mercantile Marine Service Association to become the third *Conway*.

In 1876 *Conway* was towed to Liverpool and finally came to her permanent moorings off Rock Ferry where she was to remain, without moving, for 42 years until she was moved for renovations.

In 1936 the MMSA Committee decided if they did some reconditioning the ship would be good for another 50 years. Considering that by this time she was 97 years old she was in a remarkable state of preservation. Well worth spending a good sum of money on her. The refit would have to be done in stages as the regular sequence of school terms could not be interrupted. So on July 29th 1937, at the beginning of summer holidays, she was taken into Victoria Dock, Birkenhead where much internal and external work was carried out. She returned to her moorings at Rock Ferry in September ready for the Autumn term. Having been at her moorings for 42 years, I understand there was some difficulty in disconnecting the old ship from her moorings.

A second refit was carried out in the summer of 1938 and it was at this stage that her new figurehead was fitted to replace the original figurehead of Nelson which had been lost in a collision in earlier years. The new figurehead was subscribed for by Old Boys of the *Conway* as a gift to the ship. It started as a piece of teak weighing four tons and Mr E Carter-Preston the sculptor undertook the carving. Eventually it weighed just over two tons and stood 13 feet hight. The face of the figurehead was fashioned from a deathmask of Nelson and the uniform with the buttons and decorations were copies of the original in the National Maritime Museum.

This was quite an event and it was decided that an unveiling should be held followed by a gathering in Liverpool Cathedral of all sections of the maritime industry. So on September 10th 1938 *Conway* undocked from Victoria Dock into the river and was towed across to the Princess Landing Stage at Liverpool. The next afternoon, a Sunday, a procession from the Liverpool Town Hall arrived at the Landing Stage where the new figurehead was unveiled before a large crowd by John Masefield O.M. the Poet Laureate, who was an old sailing ship seafarer and an Old Boy of the *Conway*. It was quite an occasion. She was the first 'ship of the line' to berth alongside Princes Landing Stage. The cadets, some 170, had come on board a couple of days earlier and so after "The still" was sounded on the bugle the cadets lined the bulwarks and sang the Conway song.

After three cheers for the "Nelson Tradition" the Poet-Laureate recited a poem he had written for the occasion. The senior Cadet Captain drew aside the canvas screen covering the new figurehead and Lord Derby led the cadets in three cheers for the King and read a telegram from His Majesty. Guests, officers and cadets of the ship and others then went off to a service at Liverpool Cathedral. When everyone had returned to the ship she left the landing stage and returned to her moorings at Rock Ferry. We were in Britain at that time and had I known about it we would have attended but we were on leave from China and out of touch with *Conway* affairs.

The next phase of the refit was the most difficult because at this time she had to be dry docked and the last time was 41 years ago. Considering the length of time since *Conway* had last been dry docked the underwater condition was remarkable and bearing in mind that the vessel had been afloat for just on 100 years. The whole of the copper sheeting and the felt covering the bottom had deteriorated and was renewed. Timbers were probed and examined, all underwater butts and seams were caulked and the stempiece was renewed where the anchor cables had chafed as she swung at her moorings. Some planking had to be renewed mainly in the after end of the ship.

On January 15th 1939, in her centenary year, she returned to her moorings in the river, completely refitted. Thanks for all this goes to the technical staff and workmen of Alfred Holt and Company (the Blue Funnel Line) who undertook the responsibility of maintaining the vessel in good condition in the future. The job cost £27,000 of which £21,000 was available in Conway funds and Alfred Holt and Company, generously wrote off the final debt of £6,000 owing to them.

Because of the outbreak of war in September 1939 the complement of cadets was increased from 180 to 250 and the curriculum was altered to cater for the Royal Air Force and Fleet Air Arm as well as the Royal Navy and Merchant Marine. The "blitz" on Mersey side began in March 1941 and the all wooden *Conway* was in great danger. German incendiary bombs fell on board and were dealt with and two parachute mines fell very close to her. The second one sinking a nearby ship, the *Tacoma City*.

The cadets were now moved ashore and it was decided to take the old ship to a safer place.. After some consideration the Welsh town of Bangor in the Menai Strait was decided upon. So in May 1941 in charge of two tugs *Conway* left the river, as it happened, for ever. This was an ideal place, out of the main target areas and the sheltered sailing and swimming facilities were much an improvement on the Mersey. Mountaineering and hiking in nearby Snowdonia were a useful addition to the training.

The *Conway* remained off Bangor for some eight years but the demand for training places far exceeded those available even though there were some 265 cadets now on board. The Marquis of Anglesey offered a large part of his home at Plas Newydd to be incorporated in the Conway establishment on a long lease agreement. This would mean the number of cadets could be increased to 300 and that some 100 and staff would live ashore. It worked out that new boys spent their first two terms ashore and then for the next four terms lived on board the ship.

The vessels moorings at Bangor were some five miles from Plas Newydd and obviously it would be better if she could be moored there. It would be a short tow but a difficult one as the ship would have to be towed through the Swilly Channel which was between two bridges across the strait to reach the chosen spot at Plas Newydd. The very dangerous move was to take place through the narrowest and shallowest part of the Menai Strait with strong currents. The ship had to go through a narrow gap between rocks of 91 feet and her beam being 54 feet there was not much room to play with. It was however safely accomplished. The area of greatest danger between the bridges was one mile and which took 13 minutes to pass. A new era now set in with life ashore combined with life on board.

In the summer of 1953 it was decided that the ship should be taken back to Merseyside for a refit. Tugs were required to tow her through the Straits a dangerous tow with nothing to spare as had been shown in getting her to the Plas Newydd mooring. The pilot asked for three tugs and the Captain Superintendent agreed but the MMSA Management Committee said that the two tugs used on the earlier tow would do and as the towing master was responsible - that was that. Conway left her moorings with the last of the tide. When she arrived at the entrance to the

Swillies, between the two bridges, it was found that slack water, which should have lasted for 25 minutes failed after five, and the current set against the towing party. The tugs could not manage the *Conway* and she was swept ashore on the Carnarvon side and went hard aground. When the tide fell she broke her back and became a total loss. She remained there until 1956 when she caught fire and in spite of all efforts she was burnt out. Little of her remains today, an anchor outside the Merseyside museum and her mizzen mast which has been restored as a memorial to Old Boys who lost their lives in war and erected close to the main river entrance to the Birkenhead docks as part of the Heritage Trail of the Wirral Borough Council. The beautiful figurehead now stands outside *HMS Nelson*, the Royal Naval barracks at Portsmouth. *HMS Conway* continued her existence as a shore establishment at Plas Newydd. In 1974 changed circumstances brought her proud history to a close. During *Conway's* career as a training ship, over 115 years, she produced many distinguished Old Boys who reached high executive posts in every theatre of war, on the sea, under the sea, in the air and on land. In the first World War 170 old boys are known to have lost their lives and in the second 166 were killed. In the two wars 4 V.C.'s and one George Cross were awarded together with very many other awards including one American Legion of Merit. Four old boys reached the rank of Admiral and two of Air Vice Marshal.

The loss of the Conway was a truly national loss. Just imagine what an attraction she would be moored in one of the old Birkenhead docks in her full splendour. Perhaps not as famous as Victory, but she would be afloat and would attract visitors from across the world.

Old *Conway* boys still abound and here in Western Australia we have a branch of the *Conway* Club in Australia with some 30 members. Outside the UK there are branches of the Club all over the world Vancouver, Hong Kong, South Africa and other places.

Appendix 2

FLAGS OF CHINA

In 1862 when Lay purchased seven gunboats in Britain on behalf of the Chinese Government, China did not have an internationally recognised national emblem. To avoid detention or capture it was essential that the ships flew a recognisable flag. Lay suggested a green flag with a yellow diagonal cross. The British Navy refused to accept this unless it was approved by the Chinese Government. Prince Kung was asked whether the authorities in Peking would sanction this flag. Eventually the Imperial authorities decided the National flag should be triangular with the design of a dragon on a yellow ground, head pointing towards the upper part of the flag. Lay was told that the flag to be flown by his ships was to be rectangular, green ground, yellow diagonal cross, in the centre a yellow triangle with the Imperial dragon in blue. This flag took the ships to China but when the fleet dispersed the flag disappeared but the memory remained. So four years later in 1867 the green flag with the yellow St.Andrew's cross became the distinctive emblem on all customs cruisers and floating property.

The green flag was discontinued in 1873 in favour of a triangular yellow flag with a red sun and blue Imperial dragon which was later changed to a rectangular flag of the same design.After the revolution in 1911 the dragon flag was abolished and the 5-barred Republican flag was introduced with horizontal bars of red, yellow, blue, white and black and was proclaimed the national flag. In 1912 the Inspector General persuaded the Government to authorise a distinctive flag for the Customs cruisers and the old green flag with the yellow cross was introduced as a jack in the upper canton of the five-barred flag.

The Nationalist forces took over China in 1928 and the national flag became one of a red ground with a blue jack in the upper canton, the jack bearing in the centre a white sun with 12 white rays based on a blue ring encircling the sun. To distinguish Customs craft a device was permitted in the shape of a circle with a green ground and a yellow diagonal cross in the fly of the national flag.

In 1931 the Government decided to replace this last flag with the national flag with four wavy green bands running across the red ground. The Customs green jack with the yellow cross which had always been flown from the bow of Customs cruisers when in harbour, was to be continued. This was the flag flown when the author joined the Service in 1932.When the Japanese occupied Chefoo in 1937, all Customs ships were ordered to replace the national flag with the five-barred flag and they sailed under that flag for the rest of the author's time in Chefoo.

The red flag with the white sun flies proudly over Taiwan today where it is regarded as the national flag of China, but not by the Communists on the mainland.

Appendix 3

CUSTOMS SHIPS

NAME	BUILT	TONS	USE
Ping Ching	1880	819	light tender
Chuentiao	1888	379	light & preventive
Likin	1888	270	light & preventive
Liuhsing	1902	724	light tender
Haihsing	1924	1960	light tender
Chunhsing	1927	2000?	light tender
Feihsing	1932	1000?	preventive
Huahsing	1932	1000?	preventive
Soohsing	1934	500?	preventive (light draft)
Chahsing	1934	500?	preventive (light draft)
Haiping	1935	750?	preventive
Paktau			Preventive launch
Cheongkeng			Preventive launch
Kuanlui			Preventive launch

Two more of HAIPING class were built, one hit a sunken rock off Foochow and was lost and I have no record of the name of the third.

The ships shown above were those in use during the years the author was employed in the Chinese Maritime Customs. The many big launches used on the conservancy of the Yangtze River are not listed as they do not within the scope of this book.

Appendix 4

DOCUMENTS

Contains the following documents:

1. Letter of thanks from the Coast Inspector for the author's year in his office.

2. Memorandum from Area Commander, Kowloon releasing author for War Service.

3. Author's Memo of Service. Chinese Maritime Customs. Revenue Department. Foreign Staff Coast.

<u>Private</u>.

CHINESE MARITIME CUSTOMS,
MARINE DEPARTMENT,

Shanghai, 12th October, 19 36.

Dear Briggs,

On the conclusion of your one year's service in this office as Ordnance Officer, I wish to compliment you on the efficient way in which you have carried out the duties of your office including many other duties not connected with ordnance matters such as ships' equipment, compilation and editing of 1935 Marine Report and preparation for an enlarged 1936 Report, etc.

It is not all competent seamen who are able to take to office work like the proverbial duck takes to water. You have successfully done this, and I thank you for the assistance you have rendered.

Yours sincerely,

C. Briggs, Esquire,
    SHANGHAI.

MEMORANDUM.

SOUTHERN COMMANDER'S OFFICE

CHINESE MARITIME CUSTOMS
KOWLOON & DISTRICT
MARINA HOUSE, QUEEN'S ROAD CENTRAL

Hongkong, 29th October, 19 39.

To

Mr. C. Briggs,
Acting Commander (1st Officer),
C.P.S. Haiping.

The Inspector General in his despatch No. 7389/176554 Kowloon notifies that your resignation has been accepted with effect on the 31st October 1939 in order that you may withdraw for war service.

Southern Commander.

MEMO. OF SERVICE.
[*See* Circulars No. 23 of 1874 and No. 4265, Second Series.]

CHINESE MARITIME CUSTOMS.

Revenue DEPARTMENT: FOREIGN STAFF, Coast

NAME (in full).	CHINESE NAME.	NATIONALITY.
Briggs, Christopher	白 烈 士	British

YEAR, MONTH, AND DAY OF BIRTH.	BIRTHPLACE.	MARRIED (with Date of Marriage) OR SINGLE.
1907, January 15th	Cowes, Isle of Wight.	Married (7th Jan. 1930)

Appointed to Revenue Department: Foreign Staff, Coast

On what Date.	To what Port.	In what Capacity.	On what Pay.	I.G.'s Despatch.
21.7. 1932	Shanghai "Haihsing"	2nd Off C (on proba-tion). Hk.Tls. 180+40 per month.		1674/5683 No. of 1 to Crs.

CAREER IN SERVICE (Foreign Staff, Coast).

PORT.	No. OF I.G.'s DESPATCH.	IN WHAT CAPACITY.	MONTHLY PAY.	TO WHAT DATE PAID.	No. OF I.G.'s DESPATCH.
			Hk.Tls.		
"Hai-hsing"	1674/5683	2nd Officer C (on probation)	180+40	2. 9.32	1650/5606
"Chun-hsing"	1650/5606	"	"	15.10.32	1650/5606
"Feihsing"	"	"	"	20. 1.33	1774/5928
"	1774/5928	2nd Officer C	"	15. 4.33	145866
Swatow "Paktou"	145866	"	St. $ (186.96+ 93.48*+62.32§+77.90@+46.74%)	31. 8.33	148326
Shanghai (Coast Inspector's Office) (Arms Training Course).	1873/6233	"	"	15.10.33	1894/6298
Kowloon	148918	2nd Officer C	(186.96+ 93.48*+62.32§)	31. 1.34	150490
"Likin"	150490	Actg.Commander (2nd Officer C)	$\frac{186.96+93.48*+467.40+155.80}{2}$ +77.90§)	22. 4.34	151173
"Kwanlui"	151173	2nd Officer C	(186.96+ 93.48*+62.32§)	30. 6.34	152314
"Soohsing"	152314	Actg.1st O-in-C. (2nd Officer C)	186.96+93.48*+389.50+77.90* 62.32§)	20. 7.34	153506

Port. / Ship	No. of I.G.'s Despatch.	In what Capacity.	Monthly Pay. St.$ (Hk.Tls.)	To what Date Paid.	No. of I.G.'s Despatch.
Kowloon "Soohsing"	153506	Actg.1st O-in-C (2nd Officer B)	$\frac{218.12+93.48*}{2}$	15. 9.35	158033 $\frac{389.50+77.90*}{2}$ +62.
Shanghai (C.I.'s Office)	4815/7364	Actg.1st Off. (2nd Officer B)	$\frac{218.12+93.48*}{2}$	21. 7.36	2429/7769 $\frac{389.50+77.90*}{2}$ +77.
"	2429/7769	Actg.1st Off. (2nd Officer A)	$\frac{249+93*}{2}$	15.10.36	2448/7838 $\frac{390+78*}{2}$ +78@)
Chefoo "Huahsing"	2448/7838	Actg.Commander (2nd Officer A)	$\frac{467+156*}{2}$ 78§)	1.10.37	Chief Sec Memo.8840 to Chefoo $\frac{249+93*}{2}$ +
"Haicheng"	Chief Sec Memo.8840	-"-	"	18. 4.38	170086
S.U.L.	170086	2nd Officer A	249+93*	20. 7.38	2611/8426
"	2611/8426	1st Officer	312+78*	18. 4.39	2667/8610
Kowloon "Haiping"	173726	Actg.Commander (1st Officer)	$\frac{312+78*}{2}$ 467+156* over 2 +78§)	31.10.39	176554

Resigned for War Service.

REMARKS.

Non-contributor. On contract for 6 years on terms laid down
in I.G. despatch No.1595/5491 Pens. No. 5476 Crs.

1.2.38 Appointed permanently to the Service List on expiry
of contract. Became a Contributor to the Superannuation and
Retirement Scheme. Seniority for all purposes dated from 21.7.32.

Master's Certificate (Foreign Going) Board of Trade No.30763
London, 4.2.31.

Arms Training Course: 16.9.33-15.10.33 General Classification:
A2 Musketry: Rifle 1st Class, Revolver 2nd Class.

  * Expatriation Allowance
  § Messing Allowance
  @ Shore Allowance
  % Charge Allowance.

Leaves:
```
    10. 8.33 - 14. 8.33  Sick leave
     5. 4.34 - 14. 4.34  Short  "
    24. 6.34 - 30. 6.34    "    "
    19. 8.35 - 27. 8.35  Sick   "
    21.11.35                "   "
     5.12.35 - 11.12.35    "    "
    10. 3.36                "   "
     9. 5.37 - 18. 5.37  Short  "
     1. 8.37 - 26. 8.37  Sick   "
    26.12.37 - 16. 1.38    "    "
     7. 8.39 - 14. 8.39    "    "
```

April 1934; Highly commended while in command of C.P.S.Likin
for assistance rendered in salving of U.S.S. Fulton on fire
at sea (I.G. despatch No.5415/151506 Kowloon).
Certificate of Appreciation issued by the Chinese Government
in recognition of his services while (then) Actg.Commander
(2nd Officer C) C.P.S. Likin in helping U.S.S. Fulton on the
occasion of the burning at sea (I.G. desp.No.5465/152456 Kowloon).

					Sept.		
25.7.39	received in th.$	4677.95	Retiring Allowance for	1st / ennial period,	21.7.32	20.7.39
6.12.39	"	" 188.67	"	" 2nd "	21.7.39	31.10.39
1	"	"	"	fractional and final	"	"
1	"	"	"	period of Service. "	"	"
1	"	"	"	"	"	"
1	"	"	"	"	"	"

Certified Correct:

Southern Commander, @
Main Area No.4.

Kowloon   1st Nov., 1939.

Commissioner.